The Nelson Guide to
Essay Writing

Grant Heckman
University of New Brunswick at Saint John

Australia   Canada   Mexico   Singapore   Spain   United Kingdom   United States

The Nelson Guide to Essay Writing
by Grant Heckman

Editorial Director and Publisher:
Evelyn Veitch

Acquisitions Editor:
Chris Carson

Marketing Manager:
Cara Yarzab

Developmental Editor:
Rebecca Rea

Production Editor:
Emily Ferguson

Production Coordinator:
Helen Jager Locsin

Copy Editor:
James Leahy

Proofreader:
Mary Dickie

Creative Director:
Angela Cluer

Interior Design:
Peter Papayanakis

Cover Design:
Peter Papayanakis

Cover Image:
Katherine Strain

Compositor:
Kyle Gell design

Indexer:
Noeline H. Bridge, Bridgework

Printer:
Webcom

COPYRIGHT © 2002 by
Nelson,
a division of Thomson
Canada Limited.

Printed and bound in Canada
2 3 4 04 03 02

For more information
contact Nelson,
1120 Birchmount Road,
Scarborough, Ontario,
M1K 5G4. Or you can visit
our Internet site at
http://www.nelson.com

ALL RIGHTS RESERVED. No
part of this work covered by
the copyright hereon may be
reproduced, transcribed, or
used in any form or by any
means—graphic, electronic,
or mechanical, including
photocopying, recording,
taping, Web distribution,
or information storage and
retrieval systems—without
the written permission of
the publisher.

For permission to use
material from this text or
product, contact us by
Tel 1-800-730-2214
Fax 1-800-730-2215
www.thomsonrights.com

Every effort has been made
to trace ownership of all
copyrighted material and
to secure permission from
copyright holders. In the
event of any question arising
as to the use of any material,
we will be pleased to make
the necessary corrections in
future printings.

**National Library of Canada
Cataloguing in Publication
Data**

Heckman, Grant, 1955–
  The Nelson guide to essay
writing

Includes index.
ISBN 0-17-622432-7

1. Report writing. I. Title

LB2369.H43 2002   808'.042
C2002-900465-9

Contents

- **Introduction: The Purpose of Essay Writing** — 1
- **Chapter 1: Preparing to Write** — 3
  - 1.1 Choosing a Topic — 3
  - 1.2 Understanding the Question — 4
  - 1.3 Key Terms in Essay Assignments — 5
  - 1.4 Types of Essays — 6
    - *The Critical/Analytical Essay* — 6
    - *The Descriptive Essay* — 7
    - *The Summary* — 8
    - *The Critical Book Review* — 8
    - *The Research Paper* — 10
    - *The Report* — 11
  - 1.5 Reading Academic Materials — 12
    - *Improving Comprehension and Retention* — 13
    - *Skimming* — 14
  - 1.6 Developing a Thesis — 14
    - *Thinking and Planning* — 14
    - *Common Weaknesses in a Thesis* — 17
  - 1.7 Developing an Outline — 18
  - 1.8 Dealing with Writer's Block — 19
- **Chapter 2: Research and Scholarship** — 21
  - 2.1 Establishing Your Needs — 21
  - 2.2 Your Relationship to Scholarly Resources — 22
    - *Introducing Support Material* — 22
  - 2.3 Plagiarism — 24
  - 2.4 Locating Resource Materials — 25
    - *In the Library* — 25
    - *On the Internet* — 26
  - 2.5 Assessing Resources — 28

2.6	Research Note-Taking	29
2.7	Consolidating Your Resources	31

Chapter 3: Writing and Revising — 32

3.1	Composing a First Draft	32
3.2	The Nature of Revision	33
3.3	A Checklist for Revisions	34

Chapter 4: Essay Structure — 37

4.1	The Title	37
4.2	The Introduction	37
	Context	38
	Thesis	38
4.3	The Body	39
4.4	The Conclusion	39

Chapter 5: The Paragraph — 41

5.1	Paragraph Structure	41
5.2	Transitions between Paragraphs	42
5.3	Paragraph Length	44
5.4	Paragraphing Strategies	45
	Pronouns	45
	Demonstrative Adjectives	45
	Parallel Structure	45
	Repetition	46
	Transitional Words and Phrases	46
	Ending Paragraphs	46

Chapter 6: Conventions of Academic Writing — 48

6.1	Audience	48
6.2	Academic Tone and Style	48
	Academic Tone	48
	Academic Style	49
6.3	Description/Plot Summary vs. Analysis	51
6.4	Use of Verb Tenses	51
	MLA Style	51
	APA Style	51

6.5	Using Nondiscriminatory Language	52
6.6	Basic Format	52
6.7	Record-Keeping	53
6.8	Making Use of the Marked Essay	53

■ Chapter 7: Common Grammar and Punctuation Errors — 54

7.1	Lack of Agreement between Subject and Verb	54
	Indefinite Pronouns as Subjects	55
	Compound Subjects	55
7.2	Lack of Agreement between Nouns and Pronouns	55
	Indefinite Pronouns	56
	Compound Antecedents	56
	Collective Nouns	56
7.3	Run-on Sentences and Comma Splices	57
	Run-on Sentences	57
	Comma Splices	57
7.4	Sentence Fragments	58
	Subordinate Constructions	58
	Phrases	59
7.5	Faulty Parallelism	60
7.6	Faulty Pronoun Reference	61
	Ambiguous Reference	61
	Vague Reference	61
	Remote Antecedent	62
	Missing Antecedent	62
7.7	Misplaced, Dangling, and Squinting Modifiers	62
	Misplaced Modifiers	62
	Dangling Modifiers	63
	Squinting Modifiers	63
7.8	Misuse of Colons and Semicolons	63
	The Colon	63
	The Semicolon	64
7.9	Misuse of Commas	64
	When to Use a Comma	64
	When Not to Use a Comma	65
7.10	Faulty Possessives	66
7.11	Additional Resources on Usage	67

■ **Chapter 8: Documentation** 68

    8.1 Modern Language Association (MLA) Style 68
         Parenthetical References 68
         The Works Cited List 71
         Content Notes and Bibliographic Notes 75
         MLA Essay Format 76

    8.2 American Psychological Association (APA) Style 77
         Parenthetical References 78
         Reference List 79
         APA Essay Format 83

    8.3 Other Documentation Styles 84
         Chicago Style 84
         Council of Biology Editors (CBE) Style 84

■ **Chapter 9: Sample Essays** 85

    9.1 Sample Essay in MLA Style 85
         Essay Commentary 89
    9.2 Sample Essay Elements in APA Style 91

■ **Index** 94

Acknowledgments

I am grateful to Richard Papenhausen, Doug Babington, and Colin Norman for their lessons and support. Thanks also to Jason Cawley and Sheila French for writing samples, to my colleagues at UNBSJ for their assistance, and to the staff at Nelson and the reviewers for their many improvements; any infelicities are my own. And thanks, as ever, for everything, to Sandra Bell.

Grant Heckman
February 2002

Nelson would like to thank the reviewers for their insightful comments: Lorraine Carter, Laurentian University; Roger Holdstock, Langara College; Devon Galway, Algonquin College; Ruth Derksen, Simon Fraser University; Todd Pettigrew, University College of Cape Breton; Melanie Fahlman Reid, Capilano College; Robert G. Cooper, Lake Superior State University; and Gerald Wayne Olsen, Nipissing University.

INTRODUCTION

The Purpose of Essay Writing

You may never write another essay after you graduate, but you will use the skills that essay writing builds every day. In a work environment, for example, every time you speak or send an e-mail you affect your credibility as an individual and as a professional. Essay writing makes you aware of the quality of your expression and provides practice and assessment that help improve it; while day-to-day casual speaking and writing often resemble an unedited first draft, academic writing is intended to be better: clearer, more precisely expressed, better organized, and unweakened by errors that create confusion or distract the reader from your message.

    An essay is a writing assignment, but it is also a reading and thinking assignment. Essays require you to read more deeply and actively than you normally do; you cannot comment intelligently and at length on ideas and arguments you encounter through reading, or accurately summarize them, unless you have understood the material thoroughly. Essays also demand that you think at length about a subject in a focused, methodical way; academic writing involves consciously organizing your thinking rather than letting ideas spill out as they occur to you, and it requires you to be aware of the persuasiveness of your argument and the flow of your material. So while essays develop research skills and build your factual knowledge, their principal usefulness is that they teach you how to think and how to convey your thoughts. Writing your ideas down and polishing your writing clarifies your thinking; in the long term, essay writing helps you express yourself more precisely and more convincingly in all situations.

    This book is intended to be a concise, practical guide to essay writing for undergraduate students. It contains information and suggestions about all of the basic aspects of essay writing, including the stages of composition—from your first consideration of the topic to your final checking of details of format and documentation. The recommendations presented here are based on generally accepted academic standard practices, but the final word on any of the subjects raised in this book must come from your professors; there are minor variations from school to school and from professor to professor, and the standards of greatest immediate interest to you are those of your marker.

One of the central premises of this book is that good academic writing results in large part from the writer's awareness of—and response to—the reader's needs; highlighted boxes throughout the book remind you of the reader's perspective on your work. The cross-referencing of sections reflects the fact that writing is a recursive process, occurring at a number of levels and stages simultaneously.

Remember, finally, that an essay assignment is an opportunity: to explore, to let your mind roam, to stretch yourself a little, and to produce a unique piece of writing. While there is no way around the considerable effort involved in creating a good paper, this book will clarify the nature of the task and help you to improve the finished product.

CHAPTER 1

Preparing to Write

The first step in successful academic writing is recognizing that writing is not simply a single act, but a process with steps and stages; understanding and participating in these stages will result in better essays that are easier to write. The level of organization and correctness that is demanded in academic writing requires you to do some planning, some intensive thinking, and, perhaps most important, thorough, wide-ranging revision once you have created an initial draft. Approaching the task as a series of logical steps can eliminate much of the anxiety often created by empty pages that must somehow be filled.

■ 1.1 CHOOSING A TOPIC

If you are choosing from a list of assigned topics, you need only select one that interests you and that you understand. Generally, in the case of a short essay, the narrower your topic, the easier the essay will be to write, and the more satisfying the result will be for everyone. Professors are experienced at devising topics that can be treated effectively in an essay of the assigned length, so if you choose to make up your own topic, examine any assigned topics to get an idea of the appropriate scope. If you have been assigned general topics that need to be focused, or if you are required to invent a topic from scratch, do this with an eye to the amount of space you have to work with, and what you feel you can satisfyingly deal with in that space. Check out your final version of the topic with the professor to ensure that its scope is appropriate for an essay of the required length.

When you invent a topic or focus a broad one, identify your particular interests within the larger subject, and isolate subtopics about which you will likely be able to find adequate information. Here are two examples:

Broad topic	Native Rights
Narrowed topic	The effects of BC Native land claims on the economies of the province's First Nations' territories
Broad topic	Gender in *Macbeth*
Narrowed topic	Renaissance constructions of femininity and the demonization of Lady Macbeth

■ 1.2 UNDERSTANDING THE QUESTION

Your first task when responding to an essay assignment is to establish precisely what you are required to do. This may sound obvious, but one of the most common errors in undergraduate essays is a failure to address the assigned topic directly and satisfactorily; many students answer a question related to, but different from, the one posed by the assignment, or fail to limit the essay's scope to the prescribed subject. You should confirm with your professor or teaching assistant any variation on or refocusing of the assigned topic; otherwise, even a well-written essay will not receive the grade the writing itself may merit.

Ask yourself a few questions about the assignment:

- What kind of response do the key words in the assignment demand? Focus on and fully define the verbs in the assignment that specify what kind of action you are to take (see 1.3).
- Does the assignment divide naturally into parts or sections? Does it contain more than one key verb? Does it prioritize its requirements? Does it identify central and secondary tasks?
- Is any choice provided? If the assignment includes a number of questions or issues, are you asked to deal with all of them or to pick the ones you decide are most interesting and relevant?
- If the assignment is not stated in the form of a question, can you formulate the specific questions you must answer to satisfy the assignment's demands?
- Do you understand fully all of the words and concepts in the assignment? If not, consult a dictionary or other reference texts. If this does not solve the problem, ask the professor.
- What does the length of the assignment tell you about the required level of detail? How many pages of double-spaced type does the word requirement work out to? In addition to the introductory and concluding paragraphs, about how many paragraphs will the body

of your essay contain? How many points or arguments can you effectively introduce and develop in that space?
- Does the assignment provide guidance in terms of specific resources—or kinds of resources—that you are expected to consult? (primary? secondary? recent? popular or scholarly? on-line or off-line?) What role are these resources intended to play in the paper? Is a particular number of sources suggested or required? (see 2.1)

If, after considerable thought, you still feel uncertain about what exactly you are required to do, discuss the assignment with your professor.

■ 1.3 KEY TERMS IN ESSAY ASSIGNMENTS

Analyze
Examine the structure or essential elements of something; consider how it works and its purpose/causes/features/outcomes; break it into parts.

Argue (Prove, Show)
Adopt a position and defend it; deal with possible objections or rebuttals; provide reasons for your views.

Classify (Identify)
Arrange things into categories or classes; defend your choices.

Compare/Contrast
Identify and discuss the significance of the similarities and differences between two or more things.

Debate
Present the opposing viewpoints on a subject; provide reasons for supporting these viewpoints.

Define
Identify the meaning of something; distinguish it from other things; isolate its essential characteristics or qualities.

Describe
Give a detailed account of something; depict it in words; concentrate on identifying something rather than analyzing it.

Discuss (Comment)
Present an organized, analytical commentary on a subject (using any of the techniques described in this chart).

Document (Trace)

Provide an overview of the history, development, or course of something using reputable sources to support your assertions (reference works, historical documents, commentaries, evidence, etc.).

Enumerate

List, specify, classify one by one (each point, example, thing, or instance).

Evaluate (Assess, Judge, Criticize, Critique)

Analyze the value/significance/quality of something; identify its strengths and weaknesses.

Examine (Investigate, Explore, Consider)

Look closely and analytically at something; enquire into its nature, causes, central issues; provide interpretive commentary.

Explain (Interpret)

Make something clear by providing detailed information about it; tell why and how.

Illustrate

Explain or provide proof of something by presenting examples.

Relate

Show connections and associations; establish the relations between things.

Review (Outline)

Present the key information about something; summarize the most important aspects of it.

Summarize

Restate economically, in your own words, the main ideas or features of something; give a brief account of something, eliminating unnecessary details.

1.4 TYPES OF ESSAYS

The Critical/Analytical Essay

Key assignment words: discuss, explain, analyze, explore, investigate, examine, debate, assess, criticize, critique, judge, argue, consider, evaluate, interpret, refute, prove, relate, illustrate, comment, compare, contrast

This is the most common sort of undergraduate essay. It requires you to arrive at a position—a thesis—and to spend the paper defending and explaining that position. Your thesis must be a specific, contestable *assertion*—an argument that can be disagreed with and that requires support. It cannot be merely a descriptive statement, and it cannot be a vague promise that you will eventually get to an argument of some kind (see 1.6, 4.2).

In a critical/analytical essay, the thesis must be clear to both author and reader; the thesis is usually positioned at or near the end of the introductory paragraph, after the writer has specified the subject and focus of the essay and provided any necessary contextual information (see 4.2). The body of the paper develops specific arguments that demonstrate the validity of the thesis, and the conclusion summarizes the writer's position and central arguments, noting, if appropriate, the wider significance of the thesis (see 4.3, 4.4).

One popular form of the analytical essay is the compare/contrast essay, the point of which is not simply to list the similarities and differences of the subjects being compared, but also to comment on the significance of those relationships—to make a point about the meaning or effect of the qualities you identify. The question to ask yourself is "What do these particular similarities and differences that I am pointing out *show*?" The answer to that question is very likely your thesis. All of the specific, individual instances or points that you discuss should serve this larger, more general analytical idea about the things being compared.

▌ The Descriptive Essay

Key assignment words: define, trace, review, document, identify, enumerate, classify, outline, describe

In a descriptive essay, your main task is to locate, select, organize, and effectively present information. You are responding to the information by identifying what is important and relevant out of a huge mass of data, ordering it and presenting it to the reader clearly and accurately. A descriptive essay does not usually require an argumentative thesis statement, but your introduction should clearly state your precise subject, the scope of your paper, and the principle of organization you are employing. The following is an example:

Topic: Identify and describe the typical kinds of distortions that occur in self-reported data.

Establishing scope and organizing principle: Psychologists have identified four principal kinds of distortions common to self-reported data: social desirability bias, memory lapses, wishful thinking, and response set.

The Summary

A summary is essentially a reading assignment. You do not have to invent or argue anything; you merely have to identify what is important in a piece of text and restate it economically. Writing a summary forces you to prioritize material you have read—to identify what is essential and what is expendable. The original text you are summarizing is knitted together with more examples and details than you can reproduce in your summary; often you must pick one piece of illustrative material from among many, or characterize a number of examples. A summary also requires you to view a text structurally; instead of seeing it as a collection of individual points or details, you must ascertain what it signifies as a whole—what it all adds up to. You must also ensure that you do not misrepresent the original writer's intent or emphasis and that, in attempting to condense and restate, you do not add anything that is not in the original.

Here are a few questions to ask about the material you are summarizing:

- How many essential points can the original be reduced to? How is the original organized? How is it divided?
- Are there places in the original where the author provides a summary of his or her own text—especially in the introduction and conclusion?
- What illustrative or support material in the original is essential, and what is unnecessary or repetitive?
- Is it possible to write a one- or two-sentence summary of each paragraph of the original text? Does your summary account for the central point of each paragraph of the original? (These questions may apply at the level of each section or chapter, rather than paragraph, if you are summarizing a longer text such as an entire book.)

Before you start summarizing the original, be sure you are clear about how long your completed summary is supposed to be. Calculate the approximate length of the original and take note of the ratio between it and your version (e.g., is the summary one-third of the original, one-tenth, or some other fraction?). One common type of summary, the précis, is usually about a third of the original.

If you have been instructed to write a critical summary, you are required both to summarize the original text and to present critical judgments about it, assessing its strengths and weaknesses and perhaps comparing it with related materials that exist in your discipline (see also The Critical Book Review below).

The Critical Book Review

A critical book review usually involves two central tasks: a summary of the contents and organization of the book in question (essentially a descriptive task), and an assessment or evaluation of the book (an analytical task). Many book reviews in newspapers and magazines are based almost solely on personal opinion; the reviewer simply likes or dislikes the book in question and tells you why. A critical book review is more rigorous and methodical; the reviewer considers the book in the context of other similar materials on the subject, and approaches it on a number of levels. What should be included and emphasized varies from assignment to assignment—be sure to note the specific criteria provided in yours.

Here are some questions to consider when preparing a critical book review (in fact, you should ask these questions about any sources you encounter in your academic reading and research):

- What is the book's central thesis? Is it clearly stated? Is it convincing?
- What are the major points and concepts presented?
- What is the book's intended audience? Is it aimed at a popular or an academic readership?
- Who is the author? Has he or she published other work? Does he or she have a reputation?
- What is the author's relationship to the material? Is there a conspicuous, unidentified bias in the book? Is the author viewing the material from a particular and identifiable theoretical perspective? Is the author's intention clear?
- What kind of sources does the author use? Primary or secondary? Recent? Balanced? Reliable? Popular or scholarly?
- Is adequate documentation supplied? Are there footnotes? Is there a bibliography?
- How is the book organized? Is the organization appropriate and successful? Is there too much or too little material on particular topics?
- Is the book well written? Is the style appropriate to the intended audience and subject matter?
- Does the book raise issues that demand further inquiry?
- What is the book's importance within the discipline? Is the book useful (and to whom)?

State the title and author of the book at the beginning of your review (some critical book reviews begin by identifying the text in the form of a standard bibliographic entry—consult your professor for the required style). Especially in the case of a longer review, try to include in your introduction a brief formulation of the subject of the book, its thesis, and your overall assessment of it; this assessment can function as the thesis of your paper.

The introduction is typically followed by a section of summary, and then by a section of assessment and commentary, though these can sometimes be combined. Remember that the focus of your paper is the book, as opposed to the subject of the book; from paragraph to paragraph, always be clear about who is talking—you or the book's author. This can often be achieved simply by writing something like "Gomez points out that …" before a passage of summary.

Avoid the temptation simply to retell the contents of the book. Ideally, you should try to apply your critical skills to the summary material as well as to the evaluation. Rather than neutrally recounting the contents ("Chapter One is about X, and Chapter Two is about Y"), try to give your reader a sense of why the author may have made the choices he or she did, and what effect those choices have had ("the author devotes a 30-page chapter to X, but only a footnote to Y, despite their almost equal significance"). Make frequent, specific reference to the book's content; a criticism of the writing style, for example, is best supported by a short quotation illustrating the particular shortcomings that you have identified. Support your judgments with explicit examples whenever possible. Conclude by summarizing your impression of the book and your sense of its importance.

The Research Paper

The research paper is a longer version of one of the above kinds of essays; its distinguishing feature is that it requires the writer to become acquainted with and to apply extensive scholarly material, including secondary sources (books, articles, and possibly Web sites that provide criticism, commentary, and analysis) and/or primary materials (raw data such as original texts, statistics, or historical documents). One of the requirements of serious scholarship in any field is a knowledge of the academic materials available in that field: theories, schools of thought, traditions, and major texts. A research paper is intended to initiate you into this milieu and to compel you to survey the available resources. You therefore explore a topic in the context of the ideas of other commentators in your discipline. This, in turn, enables you to assess and situate materials as you encounter them within the traditions and conventions of that discipline.

Writing a research paper does not involve simply stringing together quoted and paraphrased source materials; your research should be used to help support and develop your own ideas.

The research paper requires you to demonstrate a number of academic skills:

- the ability to locate relevant, high-quality materials on a given topic
- the ability to select from within a number of such sources the specific information that best supports and develops your thesis
- the ability to integrate quotations, paraphrases, and summaries from various sources into a clearly developed, convincing argument

- the ability to synthesize information from a number of sources, clarify connections among them, and draw conclusions
- the ability to construct and sustain an extended, in-depth analysis
- the ability to document accurately your use of source material according to the conventions of a particular style, such as MLA, APA, or Chicago

The Report

Like other forms of writing assignments, reports have recognizable beginnings, middles, and endings, but they follow a conventional pattern of sections that are identified with headings. The report format in effect provides the writer with a basic outline: when you start, you know what categories the material you need to present will be divided into, and you know what kind of information each section is meant to contain. The name and order of these sections vary from subject to subject and from professor to professor. Common sections include the following:

A Business/Commerce/Work Term Report

- Letter of Transmittal: A concise letter—less than one page—addressed to your evaluator/superior, reminding him or her of who you are, the nature of the report, and why it was initially requested.
- Executive Summary: A summary of the report, including the subject, recommendations, and significance. It should usually be about a page long—never more than two.
- Introduction: State the report's subject and purpose. Outline briefly the historical background of the problem or issue you are considering. Describe the report's scope (the range of business activity you are dealing with) and its limitations (conditions that affected your research, such as lack of access to certain resources). The methods of research should be introduced, and the report's significance should be noted.
- Discussion/Analysis: Present the findings from your research and any relevant objective information about the organization. Introduce theories or statistics that relate to your discussion, and include references to any tables or graphs (which are placed in appendices). Other headings that relate to the specifics of your topic may be useful in this section.
- Alternatives (if appropriate): Outline the advantages and disadvantages of each option. Present the option you have chosen last.

- Recommendations: Connect your recommendations to your statement of the problem in the Introduction. Provide a cost/benefit analysis and/or procedures for implementation if appropriate.
- Conclusions: Identify the significance of the proposal and how it will benefit the organization. Indicate, if possible, how the significance of the proposal can be measured. Mention possibilities for further investigation of the subject if appropriate.
- Appendices: Give each one a title (at the top of the page) and provide a source (at the bottom). Refer to appendices at the end of the appropriate sentence in the main text (e.g., "see Appendix A").

III A Social Sciences Report

- Abstract: A short summary of your method, findings, and conclusions. Present it on a separate page.
- Introduction: An overview of the problem you are considering, any necessary background information, and the introduction of your hypothesis, method, and purpose (the Introduction sometimes appears without a heading).
- Method: A description of how your research was carried out, identifying materials, techniques, etc.
- Results: A summary of the data you gathered in the course of your research, including any information on how results were tabulated or analyzed. This section may include graphs, charts, or tables.
- Discussion: An interpretation of your data, drawing any possible conclusions and raising any implications of the study.
- Appendices: Extensive background information or visual aids that would be obtrusive in the body of the report can be presented in appendices, which are designated by letter. Readers are directed to the relevant appendix by a reference within the main text (e.g., "see Appendix A").

The headings you include or omit will be dictated by the precise nature of the assignment and by specific instructions from your professor. Within the structure provided by these headings, your report should exhibit the same qualities of cohesiveness and clarity discussed in relation to writing assignments in other formats.

■ 1.5 READING ACADEMIC MATERIALS

In the case of everyday reading—for example, a magazine article or an e-mail from a friend—we know we are not going to be tested on the material, nor are we likely to have to write an analysis of it to be scrutinized by an expert. Reading undertaken for academic courses, however, does involve these demands, so students must consciously adjust the way they read. The principal characteristics of this kind of reading are that it is active and critical. Active readers are constantly questioning, assessing, looking for answers to specific questions, and placing what is being read in the context of other materials available on the same subject. Such readers are not critical in the sense of looking exclusively for faults in what they read; instead, they approach every text in a spirit of skepticism, looking for reasons to accept or reject what is being presented (see the list of questions in 1.4, The Critical Book Review).

Improving Comprehension and Retention

You must actively respond to academic material as you read it, not only to keep your thoughts from wandering, but also to help fix the material in your mind. There are a number of techniques that can help you achieve this active engagement:

- Take notes as, and especially after, you read a text. Note-taking after you have stopped reading consolidates your learning—it provides you with a record of what you have read and also tests you on the material; if there is a big hole in your memory of a text five minutes after you have finished reading, you obviously need to revisit at least part of the material, and your note-taking will identify which part (see 2.6).
- Annotate the text as you read it (provided it is yours to mark up). Writing short, concise comments in the margin requires you to formulate a preliminary critical response. Annotating also enables you to identify important passages for rereading.
- Write short summaries of various units of the text as you finish reading them. Distill each section of a chapter into a brief paragraph, and then do the same with the entire chapter and even with the whole book.
- Highlighting can also help you select the most useful segments of a text for rereading, though it is the least active way of aiding comprehension and retention. The most common error is to highlight too much of the text on your first pass, leaving you with an unmanageable mountain of material to reread; if you must highlight, select as little as possible. Look for single sentences that best summarize or characterize particular sections or important ideas.
- Use the results of these techniques to plan selective rereading. Deciding what and what not to reread compels you to assess your comprehension and retention, and also to identify what in the text is most useful to you.

Skimming

Sometimes with academic reading the challenge is not to achieve a detailed and lasting understanding of a text, but rather to digest a lot of information rapidly. If you approach every text by starting at the first word and reading through to the last one, you will never get through the material. This is especially true of surveying, assessing, and selecting materials to be used in your essay writing. Evaluating the relevance and usefulness of, for example, 10 books and 15 articles requires you to begin by skimming them to get an overview of their contents and organization.

To skim a book:
- Consider the title. What does it tell you about the precise focus of the book?
- Examine the table of contents. This is an outline of the book, topic by topic, that tells you what is covered, what is stressed, and how the information is organized.
- Examine the index. Under which words or names are the most entries found?
- Examine the bibliography. What kinds of sources does the author use? How recent are they? How extensive is the list of references? What subjects are emphasized in these sources? (The bibliography will also often lead to other relevant material.)
- Note illustrations and any information isolated in boxes and lists, or by bold or italic type. This treatment usually indicates that the material is especially important, or that it represents some kind of summary.
- Read the introduction and the conclusion. Browse through the most relevant chapters. Note any subheadings and sections. If there is a summary, read it; if there is not, read the introductory and concluding paragraphs.

To skim an article:
- Consider the title. What does it tell you about the precise focus of the article?
- Read the introduction and the conclusion. Read the first sentence or two of each paragraph. If the point of the paragraph is still unclear, read the last sentence.

1.6 DEVELOPING A THESIS

Thinking and Planning

Thinking about an essay assignment is a progressive activity: you start out with no ideas on your subject, then you begin to entertain a few possibilities, select the best ones, and gradually clarify and strengthen them. At every stage in your planning of an essay, you should keep track of where you are by making notes; seeing a version of an idea down on paper helps you to recognize its weaknesses in its current state. In the early stages of working on an essay, allow yourself time simply to think. Jot down everything that occurs to you; selecting what is useful from a collection of initial notes is an early part of the shaping and focusing process. Some planning and taking stock at this stage can make you more efficient and save you time and frustration in the long run. Itemize what you have and what you need:

- What do you already know about the topic? What are your first inclinations and responses regarding the assignment?
- What kinds of information are you going to need to gather, and where are the best places to find it?
- Can you begin to sketch out a plan of what you will need to read or reread? Is there a natural or necessary order for dealing with the material?
- What are the specific questions you will have to answer to satisfy the demands of the assignment? (Formulate these yourself if the assignment is not presented in the form of a question or questions.)
- Do you have a particular focus or direction within the topic—the first step toward a thesis—or do you need to spend more time reading and pondering?

Begin experimenting with possible thesis statements as early in the process as you can; you will need to generate at least a rough working thesis in order to make significant progress in the composition of the essay. When an idea for a thesis initially occurs to you, you must test it against what you know about the subject. Further reading, research, and thought may lead you to decide that this idea is not so good after all. You must then either adjust and refine your statement of the thesis so that it is true to the information that you have gathered, or discard it and try a new approach. You may have to engage in this process repeatedly in the early stages of planning and thinking. Keep looking for possible refinements as you focus your thinking and structure your argument into its final form, and be receptive to ways of improving your thesis throughout the writing process; the gradual shaping of a finished thesis statement can continue as you are reading, thinking, researching, writing, and revising.

One of the central activities in developing a thesis is throwing things away. You cannot use all the ideas that occur to you or every source you consult, no matter how good they all are, and you can only develop so many ideas convincingly in the relatively short space an essay provides. Improving a thesis usually means making it narrower and more specific.

Topic: Assess the safety of genetically modified crops.

First versions of thesis: 1) Genetically modified crops are not safe.
2) The long-term safety of genetically modified crops is not known.

Final thesis: Although genetically modified crops have numerous benefits, including increased hardiness and improved yields, their safety cannot be definitively established because it is not yet possible to know their long-term effects on humans or on the environment.

The focusing of a thesis tends to reveal the specific topics that you will discuss in the course of your essay. The thesis statement can sometimes include these topics:

Topic: Discuss Spenser's use of imagery in "Sonnet 22."

First version of thesis: Spenser uses religious imagery in "Sonnet 22."

Revised thesis: In "Sonnet 22," Spenser uses religious imagery to describe secular love.

Final thesis: Throughout "Sonnet 22," Spenser compares a Lover's feelings for his Beloved to the devotion expected of a Christian to God, developing the analogy through the progressively more explicit and sensually charged images of a holy season, a church, and a passionate sacrifice.

Alternatively, this information can be presented in another sentence or two:

Topic: Discuss the potential effects of Canada's adoption of the U.S. dollar as its national currency.

Thesis: Adoption of the U.S. dollar as Canada's national currency would provide economic benefits, but at a political cost. While the Canadian economy would certainly enjoy greater stability and improved ease of trade with the United States and the rest of the world, these advantages would come at the price of the Canadian government's ability to act as a sovereign power with respect to its control of economic policy.

Your complete thesis statement should, in most cases, be presented in one or two sentences. If more are required, you probably have some additional narrowing and focusing to do.

▇▇ Common Weaknesses in a Thesis

A number of common errors can make thesis statements ineffectual and inadequate. Here are a few questions to ask about your thesis:

- Does it contain an argumentative assertion, or does it merely promise to eventually present the specifics of the discussion?

Topic: Identify and discuss the principal causes of the First World War.

Thesis: The causes of the First World War will be discussed.

This example promises things to come, but provides nothing substantive. (The reader's response is, "And what will you tell me when you finally discuss these causes?")

- Is my thesis vague or too general?

Thesis: The First World War had a number of interconnected causes.

This thesis makes a statement of sorts—the reader knows that you believe the war had multiple causes, and that they were interconnected—but it is too vague to be useful. (The reader's response is, "What precisely were these interconnected causes? Name them.")

- Is my thesis descriptive rather than analytical? Does it merely state a known fact?

Thesis: The First World War began with the assassination of Archduke Ferdinand of Austria in Sarajevo and soon engulfed an entire continent.

Although this version contains more specific information, it is essentially descriptive; it describes "how," but does not identify "why." (The reader's response is, "Why did this isolated assassination lead to such an immense war?")

The more focused and specific your thesis is, the stronger it will be. In the case of this sample topic, you need to provide something that can be clearly recognized by a reader as a *cause*, such as the following:

Thesis: Although a political assassination triggered the beginning of the First World War, the conflict was essentially about imperialism and the rearrangement of competing colonial empires.

This statement discounts the importance of the popularly recited immediate cause of the war (the assassination), and identifies a specific, deeper reason for such a major conflict. We, as readers, can predict to an extent what we will find in the paper that follows: the essay writer will identify the role of imperialism in the world of the time, and specify which empires were reacting to each other in what ways.

> When encountering the thesis, the reader asks,
> - Is it clear which statement is the essay's thesis?
> - Is the thesis an assertion that requires support and explanation?
> - Does the thesis present a focused, limited argument that can be adequately developed in the available space?
> - Does the thesis satisfy the assignment's demands? If the assignment poses a question, does the thesis answer that question?

■ 1.7 DEVELOPING AN OUTLINE

Just as writing out an idea forces you to refine and clarify it, making an outline forces you to refine and clarify the organization and scope of your essay. You must evolve your own style of outlining; an elaborate, highly specific outline with several levels of headings works for some, and a scrap of paper with a few point-form notes and some circles and arrows works for others. The important thing is to be aware of an overall plan. The more detailed your outline is, the easier it will be to write the first draft—the drafting process will essentially entail turning the outline into paragraphs of full sentences.

An outline is essentially a table of contents for your essay. Start to construct a simple one when you are first thinking about the topic; as mentioned above, the assignment itself may provide you with a basic structure. An initial outline can also help you plan your research by identifying the topics you will need to explore. As you gather information, flesh out the outline and fill in the blanks. Into how many sections or points is your material divided? What kind of support or explanatory information is required for each of these units?

At this planning stage, be receptive and flexible. Your first ideas may require considerable weeding and revision, but it is better to realize this early on than to discard several completed paragraphs later—this sort of wasted effort is exactly what outlines are designed to prevent.

Keep the latest version of your thesis at the top of the page, and assess material as you add it to ensure that everything fits and belongs. In the case of a short paper, try to account for the central point of every paragraph and your principal support materials before you start writing. As you build your outline, keep track of how much material you have for each part of your essay. Is the amount of information and the level of detail for each subtopic balanced? If you tend to create outlines in complete sentences, aim to evolve rough versions of the topic sentence of each of your paragraphs (see 5.1). When you can write a solid, focused thesis statement at the top of a page followed by notes on every topic you will be exploring in the body of the paper, you are probably ready to begin writing a first draft.

If you are required to submit an outline as part of your assignment, ensure that the headings are consistent—with items of the same level of generality at the same level of heading—and that the entries are parallel (e.g., all in complete sentences or all in similarly structured point form).

■ 1.8 DEALING WITH WRITER'S BLOCK

All writers have experienced problems getting started. The first words you write always feel more difficult and more important than sentences and paragraphs you produce later on in the process. What you must try to avoid, however, is sitting unproductively before a blank page. You have to work your way out of the problem; force yourself to stay at your desk for some minimum amount of time—even half an hour. Here are a few activities to consider if you find yourself blocked:

- Keep dividing the task into smaller and smaller units until you get to one that seems manageable. What are the parts or features of the subject you are examining? Could a definition of a key term be a place to start? Can you begin to tinker with the idea you are most confident about or have the most information about? Is there a quotation that you can comment on or use as a jumping-off point for a discussion?
- Use the assignment to help you develop specific questions that you must answer, especially if the assignment is not stated in the form of a question; in the beginning, these could be as simple as who? what? when? where? and, especially, why?
- Experiment with freewriting and mapping techniques. Freewriting involves forcing yourself to write something—anything—about the topic for several minutes, without allowing yourself to revise, reconsider, or organize material. You then read what you have written, select the best idea or fragment, and repeat the process for another few minutes with the selected material as your starting point. Mapping (or clustering) is a more pictorial variation of this technique that involves writing your topic in the middle of a piece of paper and then gradually adding ideas that are related to the topic or to each other, using lines to indicate how they are connected. Writing down almost anything that occurs to you can spark other ideas and associations. At the beginning of the process,

a weak idea is better than no idea; you can improve it, reject it in favour of a better one, or use it to realize that you need to approach the matter from another angle.

- Return to the original text or source material and reread selectively, keeping the essay topic in your mind. Concentrate, make notes, look for connections, and isolate short quotations you can comment on.
- Talk to someone about the assignment. Even someone who has little knowledge in a particular field can often ask helpful questions or suggest useful approaches; sometimes just airing ideas with another person can help. If there is a writing centre at your school, see a tutor; writing tutors are very helpful about how to move forward and get organized. If you feel you have tried everything and are simply stumped, discuss the topic with the professor or teaching assistant—he or she is the ultimate authority on the subject and the person you have to satisfy in the end.

Chapter 2

Research and Scholarship

■ 2.1 ESTABLISHING YOUR NEEDS

Your assignment and the instructions of your professor should be your guides with respect to the role of research materials in your essay. In the case of some short papers, students are specifically instructed not to refer to secondary sources. This directive requires students to focus exclusively on the texts or ideas in question; all of the critical ideas expressed must originate with the student, and all of the support material used to defend these ideas must come from the original sources. (Regardless of what secondary material you may eventually consult, references to an original text will always be the strongest and most compelling support for your assertions.) Other assignments specifically direct you to seek out research material, and some even specify the appropriate number of bibliographic entries to include.

Your initial thinking and outlining will also help provide you with a preliminary sense of what sorts of research materials, if any, you need to locate. The more developed your thinking is when you begin to consult secondary sources the better. Having some idea of what you intend to say will make it easier to find materials, because there will be a defined position to which the outside sources must be relevant. Try to walk into the library looking for answers to particular questions, or information on a focused topic. One of the hazards of conducting research in the absence of any directed ideas is that you may be tempted simply to adopt some other commentator's argument; this can lead to either plagiarism or an essay that is basically a series of quotations or paraphrases, neither of which will impress a marker who is looking for a developed argument composed principally of your own thoughts.

■ 2.2 YOUR RELATIONSHIP TO SCHOLARLY RESOURCES

If you have ever participated in an on-line chat or a discussion group, you know that each successive contributor to a particular topic or "thread" has more material to draw from and refer to. Scholarship works in much the same way: it is an extended, cumulative conversation on a particular topic, conducted largely through books, articles, and conferences (it takes considerably more time than an on-line chat, and a thread can last for generations). When you read and use the ideas of critics and commentators who have preceded you, you enter into this scholarly dialogue. This means that you react to what others have said and situate your ideas relative to theirs; you might agree with, disagree with, comment on, or amplify what they have said, or you might use it as the starting point of a new discussion. What you do *not* want to do with secondary source material is drop it into the middle of your own writing unintroduced, uncontextualized, and without comment.

Quotations, paraphrases, and summaries from scholarly sources are often used to support a point in one's own argument. Quotations particularly may be chosen because they present a powerfully stated and unimprovable version of an idea, or they may be employed as part of an appeal to authority (i.e., "the following noted expert agrees with me"). Individual disciplines have their own norms regarding the use of support material. In the study of literature, frequent direct quotation from original texts occurs due to the importance in literary analysis of style and form in addition to content. In other disciplines, such as the social sciences, paraphrase tends to be the most popular form in which to present information from other sources. Your reading within the literature of your discipline will make you aware of what kinds of materials are conventionally presented as support, and in what form.

> When encountering a quotation, paraphrase, or summary from a scholarly source, the reader asks,
> - Why am I being shown this?
> - What is the precise relationship between these ideas and the essay writer's ideas?

■ Introducing Support Material

There are conventions in academic writing concerning how quoted or paraphrased support material is introduced or "framed." Essay writers can use these introductions to establish their relationship to the support material. Some verbs of introduction suggest neutrality on the part of the essayist:

> The author states/asserts/suggests/maintains/argues…

In the case of this sort of introduction, the reader must look elsewhere—usually after the quotation—to discover the essay writer's attitude to the material.

Other verbs can suggest degrees of agreement or approval:

> The author points out/confirms/notes/reveals/observes/shows/discovers/identifies/finds…

Still others can suggest skepticism:

> The author speculates/insists/claims/hazards/alleges…

You can signal that you endorse the source you are introducing by using *as*:

> As X writes, "…

Alternatively, you can signal disagreement with other introductory terms:

> While/although X claims that "…

Sometimes the introductory verb can be used to characterize the source's attitude or intentions:

> The author admits/acknowledges/grants/implies/endorses/agrees/ contends/reasons/concedes/deplores/condemns…

When you are providing a running commentary on another author's work, it is important that you make clear to your reader who is speaking—you or the author you are discussing. Keep the source's voice alive in your essay by periodically using the verbs presented above and phrases such as the following:

> The author then/goes on to/proceeds to/continues…

The smoothest and most pleasing way to introduce quoted material often involves integrating that material grammatically into your own writing:

> Bloom's status as an everyman is underlined, as Ann Bell points out, by "his comical invisibility throughout his perambulations around Dublin" (45).

These conventions are all about keeping your reader clear on your relationship to the source material you are employing. The more precise you can be in contextualizing your support material, the more effectively it will enhance and strengthen your own ideas.

Punctuating Introductory Material
- If your introductory phrase runs grammatically into the quotation, use whatever punctuation would be appropriate if the quotation marks were not there: usually nothing or a comma.
- If your introduction is a complete sentence, grammatically independent of the quoted material, end it with a colon.
- If you are using an introductory phrase such as "the author writes" or "as X states," use a comma.

See the sample essay at 9.1 for examples of these usages.

■ 2.3 PLAGIARISM

Plagiarism is presenting someone else's words or ideas as your own. It is a form of theft, and is taken seriously in the academic world, where ideas are the principal currency. There are two kinds of plagiarism: intentional and unintentional. If you knowingly plagiarize, you could fail your course or be expelled. Professors and markers have a lot of experience identifying plagiarism, and they can usually spot it within a sentence or so. They also tend to be good at finding the source of the plagiarized material (the Internet has, of course, become a popular source of plagiarized material; the same technology that leads students to the information they steal also helps professors find it). Tight deadlines and having too much to do are no excuse for this kind of behaviour; it is a matter of honour and professionalism.

Unintentional plagiarism, on the other hand, results from sloppy research habits or from not adequately understanding the rules. Here are the basic rules:

- You do not need to cite your own ideas or common knowledge in your field. This criterion requires some judgment on your part; there are a few grey areas concerning what constitutes common knowledge. Generally, if the information in question appears unreferenced in a number of sources, it is common knowledge (e.g., the Second World War ended in 1945; Paris is the capital of France); if it clearly belongs to or originates with a particular author or source, provide a citation.
- Another person's exact words—even a distinctive phrase—must be presented as a direct quotation, either within quotation marks or in an indented block (for short and long quotations, respectively—see MLA and APA standards at 8.1 and 8.2). Every quotation must be fully referenced according to the conventions of the style you are using (provided in Chapter 8).

- If you change the wording of a source but preserve the essential ideas, you are paraphrasing; you must make clear to your reader what information or ideas have been borrowed. Quotation marks are not used for paraphrases because the wording is not exactly that of the original, but you must provide adequate references. Identifying the borrowed material is usually accomplished through a combination of introductory phrases and parenthetical references (discussed, respectively, at 2.2 and at 8.1–8.2).
- A summary of someone else's ideas, even though it is less detailed and considerably shorter than the original, is still a version of his or her ideas, and must therefore be documented.

Students are responsible for their use of source materials and for understanding academic regulations, so unintentional plagiarism will also result in penalties. Read the section on plagiarism in your institution's calendar. When in doubt, supply a reference or ask your professor; with experience, you will develop a clearer sense of the distinctions involved.

■ 2.4 LOCATING RESOURCE MATERIALS

▍▍ In the Library

It has never been so easy to locate and retrieve scholarly information. Computer technologies and digital storage capabilities have revolutionized the library. Every discipline has its own tools for guiding you to materials, and once you become acquainted with your discipline's, you will find yourself returning repeatedly to the same indexes, guides, and databases. A good place to start is with your librarians, who are trained experts in retrieving information on any given topic; they will be happy to introduce you to the methods and resources available. Take a library tour, and spend some time browsing around the library familiarizing yourself with its layout and resources; you should feel at home there, and confident of your ability to find what you need.

At most libraries, you can now search for books using a keyword search, just as you do with an Internet search engine. In a library search, however, the engine scans only the library's holdings, using a controlled vocabulary of standard Library of Congress subject headings, which deliver more consistent and reliable results than do searches on the uncontrolled Internet. The more specific and limiting your keywords, the more directed your search will be, and the fewer irrelevant hits you will have to wade through. Once you find yourself in the stacks looking for a particular volume, have a look at the books around it, many of which will be on the same, or a related, subject.

Each discipline has its own indexes that catalogue the contents of periodicals; find and familiarize yourself with the ones that pertain to your field of study. In some cases they will exist in both print and on-line forms, though the paperless version is, predictably, gradually taking over. Some of these indexes, such as the Modern Languages Association (MLA) Index, include not only articles in periodicals but also chapters of books. Many libraries also subscribe to on-line databases such as EBSCO, Project Muse, or Infotrac. These are searchable collections of periodicals; they are useful and convenient, though each draws on a limited number of sources sometimes chosen for economic reasons rather than for their quality. Your librarian or your library's Web site can direct you to specialized indexes for information such as government data or newspaper articles. Every library has an extensive collection of print and on-line resource materials, including various dictionaries, guides, and encyclopedias.

If you feel you need some general material to orient yourself before zeroing in on a specific topic, an encyclopedia is often a good place to start. Encyclopedia articles will give you a basic grounding in a topic, and will often direct you to other resources in the bibliographies that are usually provided at the end of entries. Think of encyclopedias as an introductory resource, and do not rely on them as principal critical sources—seek out more specialized information. In addition to the standard multidisciplinary encyclopedias such as *Britannica* or *Encarta*, there are also many specialized encyclopedias, dictionaries, and guides, such as *The Encyclopedia of Philosophy* and *The Oxford Companion to French Literature*. Browse the Reference section or ask your librarian what materials of these kinds exist in your field.

▌▌ On the Internet

The amount of academic material on the Internet continues to grow. The use of Internet resources, however, requires much more vigilance and wariness than does the use of most materials found within the library; remember that the Internet has no standards, no editors, no accountability, and almost no rules (see 2.5). Remember also that material on the Internet is fluid; unlike the content of a book or article, which never changes, on-line information can change or even disappear in an instant. It will be a while before the Internet is as extensive and reliable an academic resource as the library.

The vast amount of information on the Internet, and the lack of control on that information, creates one of the principal drawbacks of the medium: the difficulty of efficiently finding and retrieving specific items. It is always possible to track down information using general search engines, provided your string of keywords is precise and limiting enough.

All search engines provide in their Help pages and Advanced Search options instruction on how to use such techniques as Boolean strings, truncation, and proximity operators. Two good all-purpose engines are Alta Vista (www.altavista.com) and Google (www.google.com). Directories, which offer an edited database of Web sites in addition to general Internet searches, are often a good starting point to establish the nature and breadth of on-line resources available on a given topic. The most popular general directories are Yahoo! (www.yahoo.com) and Open Directory (dmoz.org). The quickest and most efficient route to relevant academic material on the Internet, however, is often through specialized directories. There are specialized directories for almost every imaginable subject; as you explore and follow links, the same sites will keep appearing, and you will discover the most extensive and reliable ones in your own field of study.

Here are some useful academic resources on the Internet:

Academic Directories
- Infomine (infomine.ucr.edu)
- Virtual Library (www.vlib.org)
- Internet Public Library (www.ipl.org)
- Argus Clearinghouse (www.clearinghouse.net)

Government Information
- Canadian Government Information on the Internet (dsp-psd.pwgsc.gc.ca/dsp-psd/Reference/gcii_index-e.html)
- Government Resources on the Web [American] (www.lib.umich.edu/libhome/Documents.center/govweb.html)
- Governments on the WWW [International] (www.gksoft.com/govt)

Information on Academic Writing
- Purdue University On-Line Writing Lab (owl.english.purdue.edu)
- The University of Ottawa Writing Centre (www.uottawa.ca/academic/arts/writcent)

Reference Resources
- Bartleby.com (www.bartleby.com)
- Britannica online (www.britannica.com)
- Refdesk (www.refdesk.com)

Information on New Web Sites
- Scout Report (scout.cs.wisc.edu)
- Internet Resource Newsletter (www.hw.ac.uk/libWWW/irn/irn.html)

▌▌▌ Listservs and Newsgroups
- Tile.Net (tile.net)
- The Directory of Scholarly and Professional E-Conferences (www.n2h2.com/KOVACS)

Listservs can be very useful to a researcher. They enable you to communicate with people who share your specific interests, to encounter new ideas, and to be directed to new information; contributors to listservs are constantly alerting each other to new resources that are becoming available both on- and off-line.

■ 2.5 ASSESSING RESOURCES

One of your obligations as a scholar is to assess, using high academic standards, any source you consult. Students who consult a book from their library published by a well-known university press can assume that the material in it was subjected to rigorous quality controls in the course of its production and that it was chosen from among many others for the library's collection by a knowledgeable librarian. Whether students eventually judge the material it contains to be valid or useful to them is another matter; they may decide that the information is too general, or too specific, or too dated, or not relevant to the particular direction of their inquiry.

As mentioned above, however, this confidence in the basic standards that have been applied to a source is not possible in the case of many Internet sites. It is worthwhile to keep this in mind when perusing Web sites and to ask yourself a few questions:

1. Who is the author and/or the sponsor of the site?
   - Does the site appear under the auspices of a reputable academic or other institution?
   - Is the author (if he or she is identified) someone whose authority you can assess or confirm?
2. Is the site professionally presented?
   - Is the writing well edited and free of errors?
   - Is the site well organized and well designed?
3. Is the site intended for the scholar or for the general reader?
   - Is the text at a high academic level? Does the author have knowledge of, and make use of, other important sources within the discipline?
   - Is adequate documentation supplied?

- How does this resource compare with others that are available to you in other formats?
4. Can factual material be verified elsewhere?
   - Are there places, on the Web or elsewhere, where you could go to confirm important facts or statistics?
   - What is the nature of the links provided? Are they evaluated?
5. What does the URL (the Internet address) tell you about the site?
   - A .com (commercial) site exists principally to generate profit for a company.
   - A .edu site originates at a U.S. university.
   - A .org site belongs to a (usually nonprofit) group.
   - Other designations include .net (network), .gov (government), .mil (U.S. military), and .ca (originating in Canada); there are similar short forms for other countries.
6. Is the site current or recently revised?
   - Is someone keeping the site current, or has it been installed and then abandoned?

> When encountering a reference to an on-line source, the reader asks,
> - Is this material appropriate to a scholarly inquiry?
> - Does the source possess adequate, verifiable credibility?
> - Could a more authoritative and convincing resource have been found in other media?

■ 2.6 RESEARCH NOTE-TAKING

The first thing to do when you are consulting a new source in the course of your research is to record all the information you may later need to construct an entry for a Works Cited/References list.

Table 2.1 Information to Record when Consulting a Research Resource

For a book:
- Author(s)
- Editor(s)
- Title (and subtitle)
- Date of publication
- Publisher
- Place of publication

(Table 2.1 cont.)

> For an article:
> - Author(s)
> - Title of article
> - Title of periodical
> - Volume/issue numbers of periodical
> - Page numbers of article
> - Date of publication
>
> For a Web site:
> - Author(s) (if available)
> - Title
> - Sponsoring group or institution
> - Date of retrieval
> - Date of posting or revision (most recent)
> - Page or paragraph numbers (if available)
> - Complete URL
> - Any other available publication information

Record this information even if you are not certain you will use the material; it is better to spend two minutes at this point than a desperate hour in the library later when you have no time to spare. If you are consulting material that is not going to remain in your possession until you hand the essay in, record also the call number and location of the source. If you are using a Web site, print off the first page at least—the printout will contain the URL, the title of the site, and your date of retrieval.

The following are a few suggestions on note-taking:

- You must develop your own style. Some people use 3×5" index cards; others devote a notebook or binder to each essay (cards and loose pages have the advantage of being easy to reorder as your essay planning proceeds). Some write a summary of every source they consult; others record only an occasional point-form jotting or short quotation. Experiment and discover what works best for you.
- You must be able to distinguish—possibly days or weeks after taking the notes—between quoted material, paraphrased material, and ideas of your own that are inspired or provoked by your reading. Make up some kind of code for yourself, whether it be large quotation marks, different-coloured pens, symbols, or something else. This is a crucial defence against unintentional plagiarism that could doom your paper.
- Double-check direct quotations that you transcribe; they must be faithful to the original in every detail. If you are omitting material

within a quotation, record an ellipsis (...) in your notes to indicate where you made the change (see Chapter 8 for MLA and APA rules regarding use of the ellipsis). If you change something within the quotation—such as supplying a noun in place of an unclear pronoun, or altering a verb tense—note the change in square brackets; this will signal to your reader that you have, for reasons of clarity, made an alteration to the original. Whatever changes or selections you may make, you have an obligation not to misrepresent the author's ideas. Always immediately record the page number of any quotation.

■ 2.7 CONSOLIDATING YOUR RESOURCES

As you consult resource material, develop and expand your outline. Start thinking about which quotations from and references to your sources you might want to include—where they might best be placed, and how you will relate them to your argument. Add these quotations and references, or reminders of them, to your outline to give yourself a sense of how the accumulating material will work in a certain order and be divided into particular sections. Keeping an eye on the essay's required length, consider how the information might divide up into paragraphs. Look for holes in your argument or your research (are you able to anticipate and convincingly refute arguments against your own position?), and ask yourself whether your notes and research materials will provide an adequate depth of detail for the length of essay required.

As you assign material to particular paragraphs, keep an eye also on your thesis or central organizing principle to ensure that the material belongs in the paper and that all the parts can be satisfyingly connected. Monitor the amount of time remaining until the due date and the state of your progress toward attempting a first draft of the whole paper.

Chapter 3

Writing and Revising

■ 3.1 COMPOSING A FIRST DRAFT

The stages of the writing process often overlap. Some students write preliminary fragments of text while they are still taking notes or outlining; some write exploratory passages to stimulate idea production or to test out a potential direction of inquiry before they have a defined position. It is usually most efficient, however, to delay writing a full first draft until you have both a working thesis and a clear sense of how your argument is going to proceed and what it is going to include (this is part of the usefulness of outlining: the state of your outline reflects your readiness to attempt a draft). When you think you are at this stage, gather all your materials and attempt a first version of the essay. Reread the assignment carefully before you begin to write, and keep it, along with your outline, on your desk in front of you; the first draft of a paper can drift away from the topic as you get into writing, so it is a good idea to remind yourself periodically of precisely what is being demanded of you. If you find in the course of the writing that you are proving something other than what you asserted in your thesis, consider adjusting your thesis, provided the new angle is still on the assigned topic. Do not try to bend your evidence to suit a thesis which no longer seems as valid as it initially did. Be receptive to what you are discovering as you write—this discovery is, after all, one of the points of the whole exercise.

    Try to write your first draft reasonably quickly; establish some momentum and keep the ideas flowing. If you run up against a brick wall in one particular section, move on to another one. This is especially true with the introduction; sketch out an introduction if you can, but if you cannot, forget about it and start somewhere else. Start with the part you know the most about or find the most interesting; as long as you are clear on what the assignment is demanding and clear on your thesis, you should be able to write any part of the paper.

Try not to concern yourself too much with corrections at this stage. It is natural to correct a spelling or punctuation error that catches your eye, but at the first-draft stage the most important thing is to push ahead and get a sense of the whole. If you cannot think of the right word, leave a blank. If you know a section is weak, jot some kind of reminder in the margin and carry on. The more time and effort you spend polishing sections of your essay as you are writing your first draft, the more difficult it will likely be to discard or substantially alter them later when you have a better sense of the whole.

Check your progress against your outline as you go. Once you feel you are getting somewhere, return to difficult sections if you have skipped or abandoned them; try to generate something, however preliminary or inadequate, for every section of your paper. Push on until you have a version of a whole essay; it may be too short or too long, and some sections may be conspicuously underdeveloped compared with others, but you will at least have something to work on and somewhere to start in your revisions.

■ 3.2 THE NATURE OF REVISION

The revision process is not a tidying-up exercise limited to correcting spelling and grammar. Approach the revision of your first draft with the attitude that everything is subject to change: the organization of the material, the thesis, the order, the paragraph structure, everything. The writing of a first draft can in some cases even reveal that you have more thinking and research to do. It is better to discover major weaknesses in your essay at this stage than when it is handed back to you by a grim-faced professor.

Part of what you are doing when you revise is attempting to look at what you have written from the perspective of the reader. In order to anticipate the reader's reaction to—and possible difficulties with—your essay, you must try to become more conscious of the various choices you have made and the effects they have had.

The first step of the revision process should ideally be to set the first draft aside for a day or two. This will give you a bit of distance from what you have written, and it will be easier to spot errors both large and small when you return to your draft fresh and rested. When you return to the essay, try to concentrate initially on general questions such as the organization and focus of your argument. When these crucial basic features are solid, you can turn to progressively more detailed and specific considerations.

3.3 A CHECKLIST FOR REVISIONS

The following is a list of issues to consider as you revise a first draft:

- *Assess the ordering of material.* Would the essay be stronger or weaker if your second point were first? Why or why not? The more aware you are of what you have done and the more explicitly you are able to defend it to yourself, the greater the likelihood you will have made the right decision.
- *Examine your paragraphs one by one in isolation.* Does each one develop a single, clearly stated idea? Is the support material that is provided to convince the reader of the validity of that idea adequately developed and persuasive? Do any paragraphs begin with description or plot summary rather than with a statement of their central point? Is all support material focused directly on the central point of the paragraph? (see 5.1–5.4)
- *Look for ways of improving the flow of the paper and transitions between parts of the argument.* Does the beginning of each paragraph create a smooth, natural bridge from the previous topic to the next? Would transitional words or phrases help clarify the relationship between the two ideas? (see 5.2)
- *Look for unnecessary repetition.* Does the writing ever feel repetitive? Are there passages that need to be deleted or rewritten in order to eliminate that feeling? Does the presence of any repetitiveness point to a deficiency in the content of your paper (e.g., do you need to examine more ideas or deepen your discussion of existing topics)? Are you ending paragraphs with an unnecessary, formulaic concluding sentence that merely repeats the paragraph's central point?
- *Examine your introduction.* Does it specify the precise topic of the essay? Does it contain a clear and unmistakable thesis statement if one is required? Does it prepare the reader for what is to follow? (see 4.2)
- *Examine your conclusion.* Does it summarize the central concerns of the essay? Does it feel like an ending? (see 4.4)
- *Check for internal consistency.* Are the content and emphasis of the introduction consistent with what the reader finds in the body of the paper? Are there any gaps in the argument or any internal contradictions? Read the introduction and the conclusion beside each other; are they consistent without being repetitive?
- *Read the paper focusing exclusively on grammar.* This requires you to consider your sentences one at a time. Each of them must function independently as a complete unit of thought. If you are uncertain about the correctness of something you have written but

cannot quite figure out what might be wrong, read it out loud. If you continue to be unsure, experiment with a couple of revisions. Read them aloud. If a construction continues to defeat you, mark it and show it to someone else. Use but do not rely on software grammar checks; they might catch something obvious you have missed, but they ignore many errors and sometimes question correct usages (see 7.1–7.11).

- *Correct your spelling.* Use a spell check but do not rely on it. Many of the most common spelling errors are in fact correct spellings of other words—such as "their" instead of "there," or "compliment" instead of "complement"—and a spell check will not catch these. Get into the habit of looking up words in the dictionary if you have the slightest doubt about how they are spelled.
- *Be critical of all your word choices.* Precise, appropriate word choice is one of the hallmarks of effective writing. If you are uncertain about the exact shade of meaning of a word, look it up (the definition might even provide a suitable alternative). Experienced, professional writers use the dictionary constantly, checking the principal and secondary meanings of words, confirming spellings, looking for information on roots and derivations. Thesauruses can be handy, but they must be used with great care. Exact synonyms are quite rare in English; always look up the precise meaning of an alternative term you are considering. It is better to repeat the right word than to use a not-quite-right word in the name of variation; if you have a problem with excessive repetition of a term in a passage, look for ways to rewrite. Your ultimate goal is clarity, which is often achieved with the fewest, shortest suitable words; do not try to be fancy or intellectual-sounding—the result is usually a distracting phoniness. If you really want to know what a word means, look it up in the *Oxford English Dictionary* (in 20 print volumes or on disc at your library). The OED, as it is known, provides comprehensive information on etymology (the historical development of the word), variations, and sample usages starting with the word's first known appearances.
- *Examine the length and structure of your sentences.* Is there variation? A series of sentences of the same length creates choppiness or monotony, as do sentences of exactly the same grammatical order and structure.
- *Assess your use of quotation, paraphrase, and summary.* Does your essay read like a series of quotations strung together? Have you used quotation where restatement in your own words would serve as well and be less obtrusive? Are all quotations as short as they can be while still being effective? Are all quotations, in combination

with their introductions, grammatically complete? Is your relationship to the cited material clear?
- *Check all quotations and references in your text.* Is the format correct and consistent? Is all required reference information supplied? (see Chapter 8)
- *Examine your Works Cited/References page.* Is every entry complete and in the required format? Have you actually made direct use in your essay of material from all the documented sources? (see Chapter 8)
- *Check the format of the essay.* Are the margins, font size, page numbers, and title page, if one is required, correct? Is the essay within 10 percent of the assigned length? (see 6.6, 8.1, 8.2)
- *Read the entire finished essay aloud.* Hearing it can alert you to awkward passages that you might miss as you read silently.
- *Get someone else to read the essay.* A fresh set of eyes can sometimes identify problems you may have overlooked because of your closeness to the text, whether they be unclear passages, awkward sentences, or ideas that require additional support or explanation. If you have access to a writing centre, book an appointment. (Most writing centres encourage students to visit at any stage of the writing process, but having a rough draft in hand gives you and your tutor the most to work on.)
- *Proofread the essay slowly and carefully before you hand it in.* Look for small errors or inconsistencies, and take note of all your punctuation.

Chapter 4

Essay Structure

■ 4.1 THE TITLE

The title of your essay is the first thing the reader sees. Try to make it interesting and evocative of the contents of your paper. The best starting place for the creation of a title is the combination of the assignment and your thesis statement. Be creative: is there a scrap of quotation from one of your sources that you could use? Can you come up with a relevant pun? If you cannot think of anything clever, simply focus your title on the specific aspect of the topic that you deal with in your paper. A two-part title is often effective; begin with an interesting phrase or quotation, and then apply it to the content of your essay; for example:

> The Carrot or the Stick: Optimizing Productivity in the Workplace
>
> Toward the Still Point: Unity in Eliot's Four Quartets

> When reading the title, the reader asks,
> - Do I have a sense of what this essay is going to be about?
> - Has my interest in this essay been piqued?

■ 4.2 THE INTRODUCTION

Your introduction must clearly present the precise subject of your essay and what you have to say about that subject. (In an argumentative essay, the thesis; in a descriptive essay, the scope and organizing principle.)

In an argumentative essay, this information typically appears in the following pattern:

Context
- Identify the general subject of the essay (e.g., an author and a text and/or the central issue or problem).
- Narrow the subject to the particular aspect that your thesis addresses, providing any necessary contextual information (see the sample essay at 9.1).

Thesis
- State the central argument of your essay—the controlling idea that everything else in the paper aims to support.
- Provide some sense of how you intend to proceed; if possible, identify your major points in the order in which you deal with them. Try to introduce the *whole* paper; the reader should not be surprised in the middle of the essay by the appearance of a topic that has never been mentioned (see 1.6 and the sample essay at 9.1).

In a descriptive paper, you must identify the exact topic and specify the scope and intent of your essay; for example, you are tracing the development of something, or presenting a survey of scholarship on a particular topic (see 1.4).

The best introductions are concise and economical; there is no need to extend or pad the introduction. Begin directly and specifically, with a substantial statement rather than a vague generalization. Here are a few ways of beginning introductions:

- introducing a central concept or text
- stating a problem
- posing one or more questions (you should answer any questions you pose in your essay)
- including a quotation (followed by a contextualizing comment on it)
- presenting a brief anecdote relevant to your subject (which you then relate to the topic at hand)

Try to avoid the following in your introductions:
- exact restatement of the assignment, or even phrases from it
- clichés ("Throughout history..." or "Since the dawn of time...")
- unnecessary reference to yourself ("I propose, in this essay, to...")
- dictionary definitions (unless the essay turns on the issue of a term's meaning)

- plot summary or extensive description (unless you are economically isolating a particular moment in a text in order to comment analytically upon it)
- extensive background information (if it is crucial, devote a paragraph to it after the introduction)

> When reading the introduction, the reader asks,
> - Are the precise subject and scope of the essay clear?
> - Can I identify the essay's thesis (if it has one)?
> - Do I have a sense of what the essay will contain and how the author plans to proceed?

■ 4.3 THE BODY

The body of the essay—everything between the introduction and the conclusion—is a series of logically connected paragraphs that explore and support, one topic at a time, the assertions made in the introduction. The relationship of each of these individual paragraphs to your thesis must be clear at all times, as must be the individual ideas' relationship with each other (see 5.1, 5.2).

> When reading the body of the essay, the reader asks,
> - Is it clear at every point why I am being told what I am being told?
> - Does the author keep the essay's central thesis alive in the discussion from paragraph to paragraph?
> - Does the progress of the argument feel smooth and natural? Are all connections clear and satisfying?
> - Are all the points presented adequately developed? Is there any material that should be moved or eliminated?

■ 4.4 THE CONCLUSION

A conclusion should provide your reader with a pleasing sense of finality, and it should refer back to the central ideas of the essay that you presented in your introduction. The introduction, which addresses the essay's entire subject matter, is more general than the body, where you deal with more focused subtopics and present specific support materials. The conclusion returns to the level of generality of the introduction, addressing the essay's entire subject once again. Remember that in your conclusion you are addressing a slightly different reader than you are in your introduction: namely, one who has read the rest of your essay and is thus now conversant with the claims made and supported there. The conclusion summarizes the essay and brings it full circle; the challenge lies in referring back to your thesis and central points without simply reproducing them word for word from the introduction. Here are a few suggestions for writing an effective conclusion:

- Restate your thesis and/or your central arguments without merely repeating them.
- Note the larger implications of the thesis, or identify issues for further inquiry that your discussion has raised.
- Look back explicitly to your introduction. If you began with a quotation or a definition or an anecdote, reflect on it in light of what you have said in the course of the essay.
- Situate your discussion within the larger subject or discipline, or in relation to other ideas that have been expressed on the topic.
- Avoid beginning your conclusion with a formulaic phrase like "In conclusion" or "In summation." The reader should know from what you are saying and how you are saying it that you are concluding.
- Avoid using a long quotation. In general, avoid introducing any new evidence into a conclusion—that is what the paragraphs in the body of the paper are for.
- Avoid exact repetition of sentences and even phrases from elsewhere in the essay. Readers recognize any structures they have already encountered, and this creates an irritating feeling of repetitiveness.
- Avoid introducing new topics that draw your reader's attention away from what you have been focusing on and that feel like they could be the beginning of another essay.

When reading a conclusion, the reader asks,
- Does this paragraph provide me with a sense of what the essay has done?
- Does it feel like an ending?

CHAPTER 5

The Paragraph

■ 5.1 PARAGRAPH STRUCTURE

The paragraph is the basic building block of a piece of writing. Visually, it both provides relief for the reader, by breaking the text into digestible units, and signals that you are turning to another topic. Organizationally, it subdivides your argument into its component parts.

The paragraph is a versatile vessel; it can be successfully developed using many different logical strategies, and it can, in certain kinds of writing, range in length from a single sentence to more than a page. The majority of paragraphs in academic writing, however, share a number of common features. Most paragraphs include, at or near their beginning, a topic sentence—a concise statement of the paragraph's main point. Occasionally the topic sentence is merely implied or is located elsewhere in the paragraph (the introductory paragraph of most essays, for example, usually has its topic sentence—the thesis—toward the end), but it is always a reliable strategy in academic writing to begin paragraphs in the body of your essay with clear, specific topic sentences.

The topic sentence is the most general statement in the paragraph; it is typically followed by several more specific sentences that provide support in the form of examples, explanations, quotations, analogies or comparisons, statistics, and so on. A good paragraph achieves unity and cohesiveness by focusing on a single idea; everything in a paragraph should relate clearly and directly to the central point that is being developed.

■ 5.2 TRANSITIONS BETWEEN PARAGRAPHS

The opening of every paragraph in your essay except the introductory one has a second job to do: it must move the reader smoothly and naturally from the topic of the previous paragraph to the topic of the current one. This is usually accomplished with a word, a phrase, or an entire sentence that refers to both topics and expresses some sort of relationship between them. Sometimes an explicit reference to the point of the previous paragraph can begin the transition. Often, however, the connection can be merely a term or phrase that implicitly directs the reader's mind to the previous topic; for example:

Essay topic:	The advantages of an elected Senate.
Topic of previous paragraph:	An elected Senate would be more representative.
Topic of new paragraph:	An elected Senate would be more powerful.
Transitional/topic sentence:	An equally significant feature of an elected Senate would be the increased power it would wield as a result of its claim to represent the wishes of its electors.

The single word "equally" both refers the reader back to the subject just discussed and specifies the new topic's precise relationship with it. There are many such words and phrases that can unobtrusively but effectively connect paragraphs in this way. Sometimes they merely establish sequence or subsequence:

> *Another* benefit that an elected Senate would experience is…

Other choices express a specific relationship between the ideas:

> Perhaps a *more meaningful* change to the Senate's status, however, would be…

It is efficient to construct a single sentence that functions both as a transition and as a topic sentence, but a complete sentence or more can be devoted to each job:

> An elected Senate would gain more than theoretical legitimacy. It would also gain real power by virtue of its new claim to be a valid democratic governing body.

Transitional terms can be used between paragraphs, as well as within and between sentences, to announce the relationships between the ideas you are discussing. Table 5.1 lists some common transitional words and phrases.

Table 5.1 Common Transitional Words and Phrases

Adding	Illustrating	Contrasting
and	for example	however
as well	for instance	conversely
in addition	in particular	nevertheless
also	thus	still
furthermore	in other words	although
moreover	namely	even so
besides	specifically	despite
next	that is	on the contrary
again	such as	on the other hand
likewise		even though
what is more		and yet
		rather

Qualifying	Emphasizing	Concluding/Summarizing
generally	above all	finally
usually	in particular	on the whole
often	most important	that is
specifically	indeed	in short
as a rule	in fact	all in all
ordinarily	simply put	in other words
for the most part	simply stated	

Establishing Sequence	Conceding	Comparing
subsequently	although	likewise
next	granted	similarly
first, second, etc.	of course	in the same way
in turn	though	also
to begin with	whereas	
at the same time	admittedly	
in time		
later		
first of all		

(Table 5.1 cont.)

Indicating Cause and Effect	Placing Ideas in Time	Restating
as a result	formerly	in other words
accordingly	gradually	in essence
for that reason	immediately	namely
consequently	in future	that is
because	before	to reiterate
hence	lately	that is to say
so	presently	
therefore	shortly	
thus	eventually	
owing to	soon	
	thereafter	

These transitional words and phrases must be used judiciously. Avoid tossing them into your writing in order to sound more scholarly or to patch up a weak, unclear transition; use them only when they precisely describe the relationship between ideas. Be aware also of their frequency in your writing; if you end up with a paragraph that contains the word "however" three or four times, even if it is used correctly in every case, the writing will feel awkward and repetitive.

■ 5.3 PARAGRAPH LENGTH

There is no ideal length for a paragraph; the appropriate length is dictated by the nature of the topic at hand and the information required to develop it convincingly. Good writing exhibits some variety in paragraph length. Strings of long paragraphs are tiring to read; they slow the reader down, and make it easier to lose one's place. Series of very short paragraphs make the writing feel choppy and undeveloped.

The following are some questions to ask of a very short paragraph (three sentences or fewer):

- Have you provided enough support material to convince the reader that the assertion made in your topic sentence is valid? Do you need to develop the idea further with other examples, more detail, or additional analytical commentary?
- Does this material actually belong in the paragraph that precedes or follows it?

- Should the paragraph be moved, expanded, or eliminated?

Questions to ask of a very long paragraph (more than a double-spaced page):
- Is everything in the paragraph focused on a single topic?
- Is there a natural subdivision within the paragraph, perhaps where you turn (even slightly) to a second aspect of a particular point?
- Is there any repetition that can be eliminated?

■ 5.4 PARAGRAPHING STRATEGIES

Paragraphs hang together pleasingly if each sentence is clearly connected to those that precede and follow it. In a cohesive paragraph this is partly due to the fact that all of the sentences are about the same thing. There are also, however, a number of common techniques for maintaining a logical thread from sentence to sentence:

■ Pronouns

The use of a pronoun forces the reader's mind back to the noun it stands for. If a pronoun's antecedent is in the previous sentence, a connection is created back to the original noun:

> Socrates accepted the hemlock without struggle. *He* could have escaped, but *he* chose not to.

■ Demonstrative Adjectives

These, *that*, *this*, and *those* used as adjectives build connections between sentences in the same way that pronouns do:

> The attack occurred on a Tuesday. Workers who were absent *that* day struggled with feelings of guilt.

Beware, however, of using *this* and *that* as pronouns, especially to begin sentences (see 7.6).

■ Parallel Structure

A grammatical structure that is similar to a structure in the preceding sentence forces the reader to acknowledge a connection between the two:

> When the play began, the audience was noisy and restless. *When the play ended*, there was only a stunned silence.

▮▮ Repetition

Repetition of a word or phrase can create a thread of connection through two or more sentences. Synonyms or variations can produce a subtler version of the same effect:

> Revolutions do not occur only in pitched battles on the barricades. *Revolutions* of a different kind can take place in the laboratory and the library.

This repetition can also be implied:

> Four people were killed in the crash. *Three more* were injured.

▮▮ Transitional Words and Phrases

Transitional terms look back to previous sentences and forge logical connections with them, specifying relationships between ideas (see the list of transitional words and phrases in Table 5.1, pages 43–44).

▮▮ Ending Paragraphs

The logical integrity of a paragraph can be compared to that of the essay as a whole: the paragraph's topic sentence is similar to the essay's introduction and thesis statement; the paragraph's sentences of support are analogous to the essay's body paragraphs, building the argument with clear, specific statements. However, unlike the essay as a whole, a paragraph in the body of your essay does not always require a conclusion. Sometimes the contents of a paragraph, especially a long one, can be effectively summarized or characterized at its end, but often the best thing to do is simply to stop. Here are a few guidelines for ending your paragraphs:

- Avoid restating your topic sentence; it will feel repetitive to your reader, who has just read a version of the statement a short time previously.
- Avoid writing a formulaic summary or a tie-it-in-a-bow sentence at the end of a paragraph just because you think you should.
- Avoid ending your paragraph with a quotation, especially a long, indented one. Follow a quotation with material of your own, relating the quoted material to your own argument.
- Avoid putting transitional statements at the end of paragraphs; they will generally feel tacked on and out of place. Integrate them into the beginning of the new paragraph—the one that discusses the new topic.

When reading a paragraph, the reader asks,
- Is the single, central point of the paragraph clearly and identifiably stated?
- Does all the support material presented relate directly to this central point? Is the support material adequately developed to convince me of the initial proposition?
- Is the relationship of this paragraph's point to the essay's thesis or central concern clear?
- Does the writer create a smooth, logically satisfying transition from the subject of the previous paragraph?

CHAPTER 6

Conventions of Academic Writing

■ 6.1 AUDIENCE

All writers and speakers adjust their style and content to suit their audience; for example, you would use a different vocabulary and level of formality talking to your friends in the pub than you would in a meeting with the Prime Minister. So before you start to write, you must establish who your audience is. The audience for an undergraduate essay could be thought of as an intelligent, informed peer (whose representative is your marker). Such a person is familiar with the subject of your essay; if the essay is about a particular text, your reader can be assumed to have read it, and to possess a general knowledge like your own (see 6.3). You don't need to tell your reader that Shakespeare was an Elizabethan playwright, or that Durkheim was a sociological theorist, but you would probably want to note that *The Tempest* is a late romance or that Durkheim was writing in response to Marx if these ideas are germane to your discussion.

■ 6.2 ACADEMIC TONE AND STYLE

▋▋ Academic Tone

A consideration of who constitutes your audience is bound up with the question of appropriate tone. Tone in writing is like tone in speaking: it reveals the writer's relationship to the reader and to the subject matter. One of the ways that tone is established is through the level of formality the writer chooses. An essay should not be written in sloppy, slang-studded, informal speech, nor should it be conspicuously ornate and self-consciously formal. A middle level of formality—one that is precise and correct but that does not sound affected—is best for your essay. Here are a few general suggestions for establishing an academic tone:

- Avoid contractions.
- Avoid overly informal vocabulary, which includes currently fashionable expressions.
- Avoid vague intensifiers such as "incredible" or "really."
- Avoid imprecise constructions such as "a lot."
- Avoid clichés.
- Avoid exclamation marks. If emphasis is required, create it within the writing.
- Avoid excessive reference to yourself. Professors have varying attitudes to the presence of "I" in essays—some forbid it and some encourage it—and you must follow their instructions. If the essay involves your personal experience, "I" is more natural than "we" or "the writer." The use of "I" is generally only a problem when it is excessive. Your essay is about your ideas rather than about you; one way to think of it is that every assertion in your paper is, in effect, prefaced with an unwritten "I think." If your use of "I" is excessive or inappropriate, eliminate it through revision—often, the "I think that" construction or its equivalent can simply be removed.
- Avoid the second person (using "you" as a generic, unspecified addressee: e.g., "Austen suggests that you have to be assertive.").
- Avoid the first person plural as a substitute for "I" (using an unspecified "we"; your reader/marker might not want to be implicated in your statements: e.g., "Examining Kabir's views, we can conclude that…").
- Do not be apologetic, emotional, or overly assertive.
- Do not try to fill your essay with big words for their own sake. You want the most precise word—whether it is one syllable long or five. The fancier the word, the more narrow and specific its appropriate application, and the greater the chance of its imprecise use. Readers can tell when you have been overworking your thesaurus and underworking your dictionary (see "word choices" under 3.3).

Academic Style

Academic writing in general has a recognizable style, and individual disciplines possess their own conventions. In your courses you are exposed to the writing style that is typical of your discipline through textual materials and your professors' lectures. Undergraduate students are not expected to produce the level of complexity and sophistication found in publications, but all academic writers—including you—are working within the context of the available materials in their discipline, and successfully taking part in the scholarly conversation involves an awareness of the conventional style and an ability to employ it.

It is useful to remind yourself of some of the ways in which academic writing differs from more casual expression:

- *It employs a specialized vocabulary.* An important part of many introductory courses is the explanation of terms that are commonly used in the field. Being comfortable with the use of these terms is part of becoming competent as a scholar.
- *It is more precise.* The level of exactness that scholars are trying to achieve creates, in part, the character of academic prose. One element of this pursuit of accuracy is the evolution and use of specialized terms, as described above. Another is syntactic complexity: to specify something precisely sometimes requires sentence elements that qualify, contextualize, or elaborate. The result can be structures with many clauses, strings of modifiers, and elaborate subordination. Good scholars do not produce complicated prose for their sadistic pleasure; they do it because it is the only way to express their ideas fully and unambiguously.
- *It is self-referential and reiterative.* In the introduction of an essay or book, writers explain what they are engaged in doing and how they are going to go about it. In the course of a piece of academic writing, ideas are raised, reintroduced, discussed, referred to, connected, and summarized. Writers periodically remind readers of what they are being told and why, and then conclude by reexamining or restating what they have said.
- *It is highly contextualized.* Academic writing occurs, and is judged, within an environment of related information and opinions with which the reader is assumed to be familiar. The clearest acknowledgment of the importance of this context is the frequent use of external sources, in the form of quotation, paraphrase, and summary. Academic writers are constantly placing their own ideas within a larger scholarly discussion, specifying the relationship of their arguments to those of their colleagues and predecessors.

When encountering a writer's tone and style, the reader asks,
- Does the writing allow me to focus on what is being discussed, or does it draw attention to itself by being too informal or too artificial?

- Does the essay read like a piece of academic inquiry, or does it sound like it belongs to another genre, such as a personal letter or a journalistic discussion?

■ 6.3 DESCRIPTION/PLOT SUMMARY VS. ANALYSIS

If your essay focuses on a particular text, your reader can be assumed to have read it. As a result, there is no need to repeat material from the text *so that the reader will know about it*; the reader already knows about it. The only reason to recapitulate material from the text is in order to say something about that material—to make a critical observation about it. In order to discuss a specific section of a text you need to provide some contextual information, presenting only as much from the original as is required to identify it for your reader, and then proceeding with your commentary.

When encountering a summary of material from a text, the reader asks,
- Why is the essay writer presenting this material? What is it meant to illustrate? Is the writer merely retelling the original, without critical comment that depends on the retold material for its context?
- Could any less of the original material have been presented without diminishing the author's critical comments on the passage?

■ 6.4 USE OF VERB TENSES

■■ MLA Style

In MLA style, texts and ideas are spoken of in the present tense (called the "historical present"). Thus, one writes "Marx *approves* of the guild system" or "Heathcliff *spends* many years separated from Catherine." Other tenses can be used with the historical present to clarify sequence: "Telemachus *was* a baby when his father left for Troy; returning to Ithaca, Odysseus *finds* a confident young man who *will help* him defeat the suitors." If you are referring to an event in the historical past, use the past tense: "Marx *wrote* much of *Das Kapital* in the Reading Room of the British Museum."

■■ APA Style

In APA style, the past tense is used when discussing something that occurred at a specific time in the past, such as someone's completed research or your own experimental results: "Mitsumi (1999) *reported* that...." The present perfect is used to express a past event that did not occur at a specific time, or one beginning in the past and continuing to the present: "Since 1950, many researchers *have employed* this method." The present tense can be used in a discussion of results: "These results *show*...."

■ 6.5 USING NONDISCRIMINATORY LANGUAGE

A generation ago, it was common to use the pronoun "he" generically—that is, to connote both males and females. This is no longer considered acceptable; it is now the norm in academic writing to be inclusive. One of the results of this change is the use of awkward formulations such as "s/he" or "(s)he." Even "he or she" is stylistically unsatisfactory if used more than occasionally. Some writers alternate between masculine and feminine pronouns, though this can sometimes be confusing. The best solution is to use a plural noun whenever possible—and it is almost always possible.

Unacceptable   An elected official must remember that his first responsibility is to the electors.

Acceptable   Elected officials must remember that their first responsibility is to the electors.

Use gender-neutral designations to eliminate gender exclusivity—"police officer" instead of "policeman," for example—and avoid feminized forms that may cause offence; for example, use "flight attendant" instead of "stewardess." Refer to minority groups and the disabled with the words that they use to describe themselves.

■ 6.6 BASIC FORMAT

The following are generally accepted guidelines for essay format. Note, however, that your particular school or instructor may have different requirements.

- Paper: Use good-quality, white 8½ × 11" paper.
- Margins: 1" all around (see 8.1 and 8.2 for MLA and APA variations).
- Spacing: Double space (so that the marker has room to write comments and corrections), including indented quotations, unless otherwise specified.
- Font: Use a standard font such as Times Roman, Helvetica, or Geneva; avoid calligraphic fonts (the default font of your word processing program is always satisfactory).

- Type size: Use 12 point throughout the essay (do not try to disguise an essay's inappropriate length by using a larger or smaller one).
- Title Pages: APA and MLA style have their own policies regarding title pages (see 8.1, 8.2, and the sample essays at 9.1 and 9.2). Consult your instructor for variations.
- Page numbering: Number pages in the upper-right corner (see also MLA and APA standards in Chapter 8).
- Fasteners: Use a paper clip or a staple. Do not use binders or plastic sheaths.
- See also "MLA Style" at 8.1 and the sample essay in MLA style at 9.1, and "APA Style" at 8.2 and the sample essay elements in APA style at 9.2.

■ 6.7 RECORD-KEEPING

After you finish an assignment, print or photocopy a copy for yourself as well as one for your professor. Keep copies of every paper until the course is over. It is also a good idea to keep your notes and early drafts; these can be useful if the question of plagiarism arises.

■ 6.8 MAKING USE OF THE MARKED ESSAY

If an essay is returned to you with a disappointing grade, you should view the situation as an opportunity to improve your writing. Take some time to look over the corrections with care. In-depth assessment of your work is one of the principal services you are paying your professors to provide. Take note of serious or recurring errors identified by the marker. Do the main criticisms concern content, organization, or expression? You might want to keep a marked essay on your desk when you write your next one (especially one in the same course).

The marked essay identifies your weaknesses, so pay particular attention to these aspects when revising your next paper; if a particular grammar or punctuation error keeps reappearing in your writing, read through a draft of your next paper once looking only for instances of that error. Keep the major criticisms of previous efforts in your mind as you write subsequent essays. If there is something about the marking that you do not understand, ask your professor for clarification, and keep asking until it is clear; the alternative is to continue repeating an error, and to continue being penalized for it, in future assignments.

CHAPTER 7

Common Grammar and Punctuation Errors

This chapter deals briefly with the most common errors in undergraduate writing. It is by no means exhaustive—there are, unfortunately, many other kinds of errors, and, in some cases, even other ways of making the errors outlined here; section 7.11 directs you to additional information on grammar and punctuation.

■ 7.1 LACK OF AGREEMENT BETWEEN SUBJECT AND VERB

The verb in a sentence must agree with the subject in number (singular or plural: "the bough *breaks*," "the boughs *break*") and in person ("I *go*," "He *goes*"). Writers rarely make an error in agreement when the subject and verb are right beside each other:

> Molly *sews* well. (not "Molly *sew* well.")

Errors in agreement tend to occur when the subject and verb get separated, especially when the material that separates them contains a word that can be mistaken for the subject of the sentence:

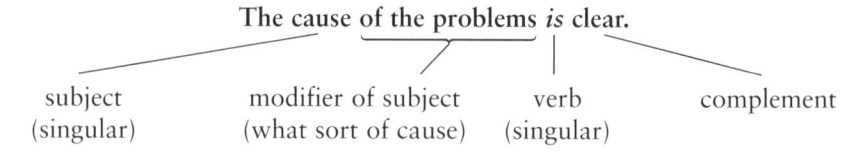

> The cause of the problems *is* clear.
>
> subject   modifier of subject   verb   complement
> (singular)   (what sort of cause)   (singular)

Guarding against errors in agreement requires you to keep track of the subjects of your sentences as you write and revise; ask yourself what is carrying out the action of the verb (in the case of the example above, it is the *cause* that is clear; "of the problems" describes what sort of cause it is). Be on the lookout for prepositional phrases (like "*of* the problems"); they are one of the most common causes of agreement errors.

▌▌ Indefinite Pronouns as Subjects

Words such as *somebody, someone, anybody, anyone, everybody, everyone, each, none, either, neither,* and *no one* are singular. This is not usually a problem if these indefinite pronouns are close to their verbs:

Everyone *was* happy. (not "Everyone *were* happy.")

Watch for modifiers that can fool you into using an incorrect plural form of the verb:

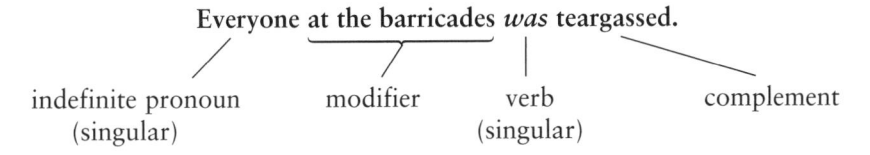

Everyone at the barricades *was* teargassed.

indefinite pronoun   modifier   verb   complement
(singular)   (singular)

Again, the key is to be aware of what or whom the verb refers to—it's not the barricades that are teargassed, it's *everyone* who is (and again, it is a prepositional phrase—"*at* the barricades"—that causes the confusion).

▌▌ Compound Subjects

Subjects joined by *and* are plural unless the two parts refer to a single thing:

Plural   The company's reputation and bottom line *are* in jeopardy.

Singular   Bacon and eggs *is* a popular choice for breakfast.

If the parts of the subject are joined by *or, nor, either... or,* or *neither... nor,* the verb agrees with the part of the subject that is closest to it:

Neither the players nor the coach *was* aware of the problem.

■ 7.2 LACK OF AGREEMENT BETWEEN NOUNS AND PRONOUNS

Just as verbs must agree with their subjects, pronouns must agree with their antecedents (the nouns they stand for) in number (singular or plural), person (first, second, or third), and gender (masculine, feminine, or neuter).

As in the case of subject–verb agreement, most errors in noun–pronoun agreement have to do with number: make sure both sides of the structure are either singular or plural.

▌▌ Indefinite Pronouns

As mentioned above, the words that end in *-body*, *-one*, or *-thing* (see 7.1) are singular; so are *one*, *each*, *either*, *neither*, *none*, and *no one*.

> Each of the girls exhibited *her* own style. (each one of the girls)
>
> None of the dogs had lost *its* collar. (none = not one)

In conversation, it is common to use a plural pronoun with some indefinite pronouns:

> Everyone in the club submitted *their* best work.

In academic writing, however, the more correct singular form is still the norm:

> Everyone in the club submitted *his or her* best work.

If this seems awkward, it is always possible to rewrite:

> All of the club's members submitted *their* best work.

▌▌ Compound Antecedents

When a pronoun refers to two or more singular nouns joined by *and*, the pronoun must be plural:

> Janis and Edouardo took a taxi because *their* car wouldn't start.

If the singular nouns are joined by *or* or *nor*, the pronoun is singular:

> Neither John nor Bill could find *his* racquet.

If one noun is singular and the other is plural, put the plural one second and make the pronoun plural:

> Neither the boss nor the employees were happy with *their* jobs.

▌▌ Collective Nouns

Some words can be either singular or plural, depending on how they are used:

> The team won *its* fourth consecutive game. (the team is spoken of as a single unit)

> The team conveyed *their* best wishes on the get-well-quick card. (the team is spoken of as a number of individuals with different "best wishes")

Other examples of compound nouns are *family, committee, class, couple,* and *audience*. Watch out for singular nouns that can be confusing because of their form or because they refer to a thing that has many parts or members:

> The United States protects *its* interests internationally.
>
> The government was responsible for *its* own defeat.

In cases like this, the immediate clue is that you naturally choose the singular form of the verb to go with such nouns—few people would be tempted to write "The current government *are* a good one."

■ 7.3 RUN-ON SENTENCES AND COMMA SPLICES

In the case of both run-on sentences and comma splices, two complete sentences—two independent clauses—are punctuated as if they were a single sentence.

▋▋ Run-on Sentences

A run-on sentence is two complete sentences run together without any punctuation between them:

> I read the paper this morning it was raining at the time.

This lack of adequate punctuation interferes with the clarity of the writing. A strong mark of division (which we convey in speech with pause and inflection) is required between the two thoughts; if it is not there, the reader can become momentarily confused.

▋▋ Comma Splices

A comma splice is two complete sentences joined only by a comma, which is an inadequate mark of division for that kind of construction:

> The summer was over, people were bringing out their warmer clothes.

Run-on sentences and comma splices can be fixed in a number of ways:

1. Use a semicolon between the two sentences to indicate that there is an important connection between the two thoughts (see 7.8):

   > The summer was over; people were bringing out their warmer clothes.

2. Use both a comma and a coordinating conjunction (*and, but, for, yet, so, or, nor*):

   The summer was over, *and* people were bringing out their warmer clothes.

3. Use a period:

   The summer was over. People were bringing out their warmer clothes.

4. Turn one of the sentences into a subordinate clause:

   Because the summer was over, people were bringing out their warmer clothes.

Note: Use a semicolon, not a comma, when you are joining two complete sentences with words like *however, therefore, thus, moreover, rather, instead, furthermore, indeed,* or *also*. These words are conjunctive adverbs, and they do not perform the same grammatical function as coordinating conjunctions (of which there are only seven—see above). One way to distinguish between these two parts of speech is that a conjunctive adverb, because it is a modifier, can be placed elsewhere in the second sentence, whereas a conjunction cannot be relocated. Insert a comma after conjunctive adverbs that are placed between sentences.

> Hockney insists that artists such as Vermeer routinely used optical devices in the execution of their work; however, many art historians reject this theory.

■ 7.4 SENTENCE FRAGMENTS

A correct sentence expresses a complete thought. A sentence fragment is a partial sentence—an incomplete thought—punctuated as if it were a complete sentence. Most fragments fall into two categories: subordinate constructions and phrases.

■■ Subordinate Constructions

Many of the sentences that we write contain a part that makes sense on its own and a part that does not. Consider the following example:

> Although it was raining, I headed out to play tennis.

It is possible to write "I headed out to play tennis" on its own as a sentence—it is a complete thought. It is not possible to write only "Although it was raining." This clause (a group of words containing a subject and a verb) is incomplete: it depends on "I headed out to play tennis" to make sense. It is a *subordinate* or *dependent* clause. Many of the sentence fragments in student writing are merely subordinate clauses without a *main* or *independent* clause to complete them. They can often be corrected simply by being joined to the sentence that precedes or follows them.

Subordinate clauses begin with a word or phrase that makes them subordinate (notice in the example above—"Although it was raining"—that if you take off the first word, "although," what's left is a complete sentence). Here are the most common subordinating conjunctions:

after	even though	though	wherever
although	if	unless	whereas
as	if only	until	whether
as though	once	whatever	while
because	rather than	whenever	
before	since	whereas	

Try to be aware of the presence of these words in your writing. Any clause that begins with one of these words used as a conjunction is going to be incomplete and dependent on an accompanying independent clause to create a satisfying, whole sentence.

▌▌ Phrases

▌▌▌ Verbal Phrases

Verbs in their *-ing* form (e.g., *being, going*) cannot serve as whole, complete verbs on their own—they always appear, when they are used as verbs, with helping verbs that are a form of the verb *to be* (e.g., You *are being* unhelpful; I *am going* home). When these *-ing* forms appear on their own, they are always part of constructions that function as other parts of speech:

> We went to the restaurant. Being hungry at the time.

In this example, "being hungry at the time" functions as an adjective modifying "we." The phrase does not make sense on its own; it needs to be connected (with a comma) to the independent clause that precedes it—"We went to the restaurant"—which does make sense on its own.

Be on the lookout for other such incomplete phrases that need the independent clause before or after them in order to make sense.

▌▌▌ Prepositional Phrases

Fragment	The government created tax breaks. For the lower class.
Correction	The government created tax breaks for the lower class.

Appositive Phrases

Fragment   My favourite singer is Björk. A woman who has had a difficult life.

Correction My favourite singer is Björk, a woman who has had a difficult life.

Noun Phrases

Fragment   Hundreds of new drugs to combat AIDS. They created hope of a cure.

Correction Hundreds of new drugs to combat AIDS created hope of a cure.

■ 7.5 FAULTY PARALLELISM

Parallelism refers to the arrangement of elements within a sentence in a similar, compatible form. The elements that are parallel can be words, phrases, or clauses. One of the most common examples of parallelism is the list, within which items should be presented in a consistent way:

Incorrect   Janis is young, carefree, and a rebel.

The writer of this sentence establishes a pattern—describing Janis as "young" (an adjective) and "carefree" (an adjective)—and then violates that pattern by making the third element a noun ("rebel"). By the time the second adjective appears, the reader has picked up the pattern, and is expecting another adjective; a noun in its place feels wrong, and perhaps causes momentary confusion. (What is the wrong kind of word doing there? Did I miss something?) The sentence is more satisfying if the structure is parallel:

Correct   Janis is young, carefree, and rebellious. (three adjectives)

Whenever you provide a list of any kind—after a colon, in point form, or in a numbered sequence—be sure that all of the elements are expressed in a consistent form. Also ensure that the phrases and clauses that are presented in a parallel way are consistent:

Incorrect   He was accused of embezzling funds, abusing the expense account, and theft of merchandise.

Again, the writer establishes a pattern—the use of the *-ing* form (*embezzling, abusing*)—and then violates that pattern by using the noun "theft."

Correct   He was accused of embezzling funds, abusing the expense account, and stealing merchandise.

Another common error involves the use of "that":

Incorrect	The author claims that the studies were inconclusive, that the researchers lied, and the university attempted a cover-up.

If the first two of the three claims are introduced with "that," then the third one must be too:

Correct	The author claims that the studies were inconclusive, that the researchers lied, and that the university attempted a cover-up.

■ 7.6 FAULTY PRONOUN REFERENCE

Because pronouns refer to and stand for nouns (their *antecedents*), it must always be clear which noun is the intended antecedent. This section discusses four common errors in pronoun reference: ambiguous reference, vague reference, remote antecedent, and missing antecedent.

■■ Ambiguous Reference

Watch out for situations in which there are two or more possible antecedents for a pronoun:

> Sue met Esme when she was working at the theatre.

Which one was working at the theatre? You must either supply the clarifying noun or, preferably, rewrite the sentence:

> Sue was working at the theatre when Esme met her.

■■ Vague Reference

Beware of starting sentences with the word "this." Confusion can result if there is more than one possible reference for the "this":

> Danica arrived without apology an hour late for their meeting and informed Greg that she had sold the house. This enraged him.

What enraged him? That she was late? That she sold the house? The best revision in this situation is usually to supply a clarifying noun after "this":

> This discourteous behaviour enraged him.

> This news enraged him.

If you find yourself beginning a number of sentences with "this," revise them to eliminate the word.

▐▌ Remote Antecedent

When you encounter a pronoun in your reading, you subconsciously look for the closest suitable noun that will serve as an antecedent:

> The political problems in the country continued to multiply, and the markets reflected the citizens' anxiety. Many began to invest in foreign stocks. *They* could be solved, but only through a return to democratic principles.

The phrase "political problems," to which "they" refers, is too far away from the pronoun, and the reader has to hunt around to make the connection.

▐▌ Missing Antecedent

Ensure that the noun to which a pronoun is intended to refer is actually present:

> In Charles Dickens's *Hard Times*, he focuses on the role of education.

"He" refers to "Charles Dickens," but in fact "Charles Dickens" has not been mentioned—only his book has ("Charles Dickens's" functions as an adjective, modifying *Hard Times*):

> In *Hard Times*, Charles Dickens focuses on the role of education.

■ 7.7 MISPLACED, DANGLING, AND SQUINTING MODIFIERS

Just as pronouns must clearly refer to particular nouns, modifiers must clearly refer to the sentence element that they are intended to modify. Problems with misplaced, dangling, and squinting modifiers can usually be solved by moving the modifier closer to the thing it applies to.

▐▌ Misplaced Modifiers

Modifiers can often be placed in a number of locations within a sentence. Ensure that the placement you choose creates the desired meaning:

Misplaced   We saw the battlefield where Wolfe died last year.

Wolfe did not die last year; you saw the battlefield last year. Moving the modifier closer to "we saw" eliminates the problem:

Clear   Last year, we saw the battlefield where Wolfe died.

Sometimes the change in meaning that results from relocating a modifier is subtle:

Misplaced   The professor not only failed the cheater but also the student who supplied the answers.

In this sentence "not only" seems to apply to the verb "failed"; the reader would expect another verb after "but also" (e.g., "The professor not only *failed* the cheater, but also *reported* him to the Dean."). Moving "not only" closer to the element it refers to clarifies the meaning:

Clear   The professor failed not only the cheater but also the student who supplied the answers.

■ Dangling Modifiers

A dangling modifier is a word, phrase, or clause that has nothing in the sentence to attach itself to; the thing or person that it seems to want to name never gets mentioned:

> Walking by the seashore, the tide began to come in.

It sounds like the tide was walking. The missing agent is whoever was walking by the seashore. Supplying that information solves the problem:

> Walking by the seashore, we watched the tide come in.

> While I was walking by the seashore, the tide began to come in.

When your sentence begins with a construction like this one, ask yourself who or what is performing the action and name that agent.

■ Squinting Modifiers

A squinting modifier can refer to either of two elements in a sentence:

> Beer stores are closed on Sundays only in New Brunswick.

Are they closed one day only in New Brunswick, or is New Brunswick the only province in which they are closed on Sundays? Reordering the sentence eliminates the ambiguity:

> In New Brunswick, beer stores are closed only on Sundays.

> Only in New Brunswick are beer stores closed on Sundays.

■ 7.8 MISUSE OF COLONS AND SEMICOLONS

■ The Colon

The colon is used at the end of a complete sentence to introduce a list, a quotation, or an explanation:

> There were three people at the meeting: Ping, Helen, and Juanita.
>
> Oscar Wilde said it best: "I can resist anything but temptation."
>
> Greenhouse gases have an identifiable effect on weather patterns: they contribute to global warming.

Avoid using a colon in the middle of a sentence:

Incorrect	The three people at the meeting were: Ping, Helen, and Juanita.
Correct	The three people at the meeting were Ping, Helen, and Juanita.

The Semicolon

The semicolon is a mark of division. It has two principal uses: between related, complete sentences, and between long or complex elements of a list.

1. Between related sentences
   Two complete sentences that are closely related can be separated by a semicolon rather than by a period:

   > I asked Molly to the dance; she said she'd rather stay at home.

   Ensure that the structure on each side of the semicolon could function as an independent sentence on its own.

2. Between elements of a list
   If the individual elements of a list are very long, or if they contain internal punctuation, use a semicolon to clarify the grouping of elements:

   > There were three people at the meeting: Ping, the secretary; Helen, the president; and Juanita, the treasurer.

7.9 MISUSE OF COMMAS

A comma creates a slight pause, helping to clarify meaning by separating words, phrases, and clauses.

When to Use a Comma

- When you join two complete sentences with a coordinating conjunction (*and, but, for, yet, so, or, nor*), put a comma *before* the conjunction:

  > We started the evening at the restaurant, *and* later we went to the concert.

The comma can be omitted if the two sentences are very short and closely related:

> I liked the movie and she hated it.

- Commas are used to set off elements that interrupt the sentence, introductory elements, elements of a list, and subordinate clauses:

Interruptions	The practical guitarist, who began his career in a punk band, had moved on to country.
Introductory elements	Unfortunately, his guitar was always too loud. After one particularly blistering solo, he was fired.
Elements of a list	He lost his house, his wife, his truck, and his dog.
Subordinate clauses	Although he had wanted to be a country guitarist, he became a songwriter instead.

When Not to Use a Comma

- Do not place a comma between the subject and verb of a sentence, even if the subject and its modifiers seem long:

Incorrect	The problem of how best to prevent the further shrinking of the Amazon rain forest, was addressed at the conference.
Correct	The problem of how best to prevent the further shrinking of the Amazon rain forest was addressed at the conference.

Commas may be used between the subject and verb of a sentence to mark off an interruption—usually a word or phrase that renames the subject, but that is not essential to the subject's meaning (called a nonrestrictive appositive):

> The airplane, a Second World War Lancaster bomber, was being restored.

If the appositive is necessary for the meaning of the subject to be clear (if it identifies *which one*), use no commas:

> The film *Citizen Kane* is considered by many to be a classic.

- Do not use a comma before the first item in a series:

Incorrect	The three topics addressed by the speaker were, pride, civic duty, and hope.

Correct   The three topics addressed by the speaker were pride, civic duty, and hope.

■ 7.10 FAULTY POSSESSIVES

Nouns that end in -s can be singular, plural, or possessive; it is important to punctuate them properly to avoid confusion. The first step is to be sure that you are distinguishing between plurals and possessives. When you write a noun that ends in -s, ask yourself whether the meaning you intend is *more than one* of that noun or *something belonging* to that noun:

Plural   the angry dogs bark (more than one angry dog barks)

To form the singular possessive, add an apostrophe and the letter *s* to the singular noun:

Possessive   the angry dog's bark (the bark belonging to the angry dog)

To form the plural possessive, add only an *apostrophe* to the plural noun:

Plural possessive   the angry dogs' bark (the bark belonging to the angry dogs)

If the plural noun does not end in -s, add an apostrophe + s:

The children's room

The people's representative

An apostrophe + *s* is also added in most cases if the singular noun ends in -s:

The class's work

Bridget Jones's Diary

Some writers add only the apostrophe in cases where the final -s would create an awkward pronunciation:

Jesus' teachings

Euripides' plays

In the case of a compound noun, add an apostrophe only after the last noun if the nouns are truly functioning together as a compound:

Fatima and Eric's car broke down. (one car belonging to the two of them as a unit)

Fatima's and Eric's memories of the honeymoon are very different. (multiple, different memories belonging to each of them individually)

Possessive pronouns are an exception to the rule. The most common error involving possession is made in the case of the word *its*:

its = belonging to it (possessive; do not use an apostrophe)

The team has changed *its* uniform.

it's = it is or it has (contraction; use an apostrophe)

It's starting to rain.

Apostrophes are never used with any of the possessive pronouns (*hers, his, theirs, yours, ours, its*).

■ 7.11 ADDITIONAL RESOURCES ON USAGE

In addition to the usage guides available in your library, the Internet provides a great deal of information at no cost; you can find help on almost any topic in the form of explanatory text, printable handouts, and exercises. Here are some sites that offer extensive resources relating to grammar and punctuation:

- Purdue University's OWL (On-line Writing Lab) <owl.english.purdue.edu> offers more than a hundred handouts on grammar, documentation and ESL issues.
- The University of Victoria's Hypertext Writer's Guide <web.uvic.ca/wguide> contains extensive information on grammar and on the study of literature.
- Guide to Grammar and Style by Jack Lynch <www.andromeda.rutgers.edu/~jlynch/Writing> presents extensive explanatory information on usage and links to other sites.

If you find yourself in frequent need of reference information on usage, invest in a handbook. There are a great many available, all containing similar information (some also include specialized content, such as ESL tips or advice for professional writers). Here are a couple of popular general guides:

- DiYanni, Robert, and Pat C. Hoy II. *The Scribner Handbook for Writers*. Needham Heights, MA: Allyn and Bacon, 2001.
- Hacker, Diana. *A Canadian Writer's Reference*. Scarborough, ON: Nelson Thomson Learning, 2001.

CHAPTER 8

Documentation

Documentation serves two main purposes: it enables you to acknowledge your debt to other writers whose ideas you have used in quotations, paraphrases, and summaries; and it provides the information necessary to lead your reader to those sources. The rules may seem finicky, but they exist to create an unambiguous standard form that can be clearly understood by all readers.

■ 8.1 MODERN LANGUAGE ASSOCIATION (MLA) STYLE

The following information is based on the *MLA Handbook for Writers of Research Papers*, 5th ed. (New York: MLA, 1999) and on material found at the Modern Language Association's Web site <www.mla.org>.

▌▌ Parenthetical References

Reference to source material within the text of your essay must be cited. Except in the case of some historians who still employ the Chicago style (see 8.3), the system of footnotes or endnotes has given way to systems of in-text, parenthetical citations. This in-text citation performs two functions: it identifies the source and acknowledges the original author's contribution; and it directs your reader to a particular entry in your Works Cited list, which contains additional information on the source. The two pieces of information you must provide within your text, if they are available, are the author's name(s) and a page number. Usually this is accomplished with a combination of an introductory phrase (see 2.2) and a parenthetical reference at the end of the source material:

> Austin Lowe notes that these regulations "have the effect of discouraging variety and experimentation in documentary programming" (43).

If the author's name is not provided in an introductory phrase, it is included within the parentheses:

> These regulations have been seen to impede free experimentation within the medium (Lowe 43).

A Note on Punctuation
- The period is placed after the parenthesis (the parenthetical material belongs to the sentence that precedes it). However, when a long quotation is indented and set off from the main text, the parenthesis follows the final period.
- If the quoted material ends with a question mark or an exclamation point, that punctuation is included at the end of the quotation, and the parenthesis is still followed by a period.
- The author's name is followed by a space and the page number, which appears without "page" or "p."

Multiple Authors

If the source has two or three authors, name them in the introductory phrase or in the parenthetical citation:

> (Aziz, Cranston, and Gomez 132)

If there are more than three authors, use the first author's name plus the phrase "et al." ("and others"):

> (Joyce et al. 99)

Corporate Author

When the author is an organization, identify it in the introductory phrase or include its name—or a shortened version of the name—in a parenthetical citation to guide your reader to the relevant entry in your Works Cited page:

> A UNESCO report confirms that "the number of deaths from malnutrition in sub-Saharan Africa is on the rise" (68).

> Meanwhile, the death toll from malnutrition in sub-Saharan Africa continues to climb (UNESCO 68).

Author Unknown

If no author is specified in the original, use the title of the work in your introductory phrase or one or two identifying words from the title in a parenthetical citation (beginning with the word by which it is alphabetized in your Works Cited list):

> The number of illegal downloads increased more than ten-fold within a single year ("Beyond Napster" 55).

Present the identifying words from the title in the form in which they appear in your Works Cited list (e.g., in quotation marks for the title of a shorter text, in italics or underlined for a full-length text).

Multivolume Works

Include the relevant volume number with the page number in the parenthetical citation:

> (Bloom 3:44)

Literary Works

In the case of a play, supply act, scene, and line numbers, as applicable:

> Prospero reflects sadly on Miranda's wonder: "'Tis new to thee" (5.1.189).

In the case of a short poem, provide line numbers:

> Shakespeare ends the sonnet with a reminder of our mortality: "This thou perceivest, which makes thy love more strong, / To love that well which thou must leave ere long" (13–14).

If the poem is in books or parts, cite the part as well as the line numbers:

> Milton's aim in *Paradise Lost* is to "justify the ways of God to men" (1.26).

Works in an Anthology

The name in the introductory phrase or parenthetical citation should always be the author of the work referred to, not that of an editor or of another author who quotes it; this reflects the fact that the corresponding Works Cited entry begins with—and is alphabetized according to—the name of the author, not the editor.

Indirect Sources

Try to cite from original sources. If you must quote or refer to an author's words that you found in a source written by a third party, include the notation "qtd. in" ("quoted in") in the parenthetical citation:

> Markus contends that "this era of Dutch hospitality ended with the onset of World War II" (qtd. in Crossfield 56).

Electronic Sources

If possible, provide an author and a page number as you would for a print source. If there are no page numbers, supply a paragraph number (using the abbreviation "par." or "pars.") or a screen number, if either of these is available—if not, omit the number. If there is no specified author, and the site is listed by title on your Works Cited page, include all or part of the title in your parenthetical citation.

The Works Cited List

The Works Cited list contains detailed entries for all of the sources you have cited in your essay; these entries provide titles, subtitles, dates of publication, publishers, places of publication, editors, and other relevant information about your sources. Do not include works not directly referred to in the essay.

Here are some of the essential features of the Works Cited list:

- It appears on its own page (or pages) after the main text of your essay.
- The words "Works Cited" appear centred one inch from the top of the page, in the same font and text size as the body of your paper, and in plain text—not underlined or in bold or in quotation marks.
- The entries are alphabetized by the authors' or editors' last names. If there is no author, alphabetize the entry according to the first word of the title (excluding the articles *a*, *an*, or *the*).
- The first line of each entry begins at the standard left-hand margin, and any subsequent lines are indented five spaces (or one-half inch). This makes it easier for the reader to skim down the list and find a particular entry.

See the Works Cited page of the sample essay at 9.1.

Format of Works Cited List Entries

- A basic Works Cited entry for a book is divided into three parts, separated by periods: the author (last name first), the title (and the subtitle, if there is one), and the publication information (place of publication, colon, publisher, comma, year of publication, period).
- Titles of full-length works—books, plays, long poems such as *The Odyssey* or *The Prelude*, periodicals, newspapers, pamphlets, films, television or radio programs, operas, recordings, works of art—are presented either in italics or underlined; be consistent.
- Titles of shorter works and works published within larger works—articles, short stories, chapters, essays, short poems, songs, individual episodes of a television or radio series, lectures, speeches—are presented in quotation marks.

- If the place of publication is not a major city, include the state, province, or country: (Scarborough, ON: Nelson Canada, 1998).
- The publisher's name can be shortened (you can generally eliminate articles, abbreviations and descriptive words like "Press" or "Publishers"—but keep the word "Press" in the case of university presses).
- Use the most recent copyright date provided.
- Take your information from the book's title page and copyright page.

Models of Works Cited Entries

Book
Author's Last Name, First Name. *Title of Book: Subtitle of Book.* Place of Publication: Publisher, Year of Publication.

Article
Author's Last Name, First Name. "Title of Article." *Title of Periodical* Volume (Year): Page Numbers of Article.

Web Page
Author's Last Name, First Name. *Title of Site.* Date of Posting or Revision. Sponsoring Organization or Institution. Date of Access <URL>.

Note: See "Sample Electronic Source Entries" on page 74, which provides more detail concerning the types of information that can appear in a citation for an on-line source.

Sample Book Entries

Book with One Author
Bell, Sandra. *Courting the Muse: Poetry and Politics in the Courts of King James I and VI.* Vancouver: Isherwood, 2002.

Book with Two or Three Authors
Johnston, Nancy, and Connie Holland. *An Integrated Approach to ESL Instruction.* London: Faber and Faber, 2000.

Note: Only the first author is presented last name first.

Book with Four or More Authors
Sleep, Renea, et al. *Educational Funding in Canada.* Calgary: University of Alberta Press, 2001.

Book with an Editor
Flanagan, Richard, ed. *The Tao of the Saxophone.* Kingston, ON: Quarry, 2000.

Note: If there is more than one editor, use "eds."

Book with an Unknown Author
    A Short History of Nova Scotia. Halifax: Deep Sea, 1989.

Note: When alphabetizing by title, ignore the articles *A*, *An*, and *The*. Thus, this entry would be alphabetized under *S* for *Short*.

Book with a Corporate or Governmental Author
    Statistics Canada. *Report on Child Poverty*. Ottawa: Statistics Canada, 2002.

Note: The corporate author is cited even if it is also the publisher.

Work in an Anthology
    Marlowe, Christopher. "The Passionate Shepherd to His Love." *The Norton Anthology of English Literature*. 7th edition. Ed. M.H. Abrams. Vol. 1. New York: Norton, 2001. 278–279.

Foreword, Preface, Introduction, or Afterword
    Sakell, Michael. Preface. *The Permanence of Greek Culture*. By Kostas Dragonas. Toronto: Bellwether, 1997. i–xii.

Note: Present page numbers in the form in which they appear in the original; in this case, roman numerals.

Sample Article Entries

Article in a Journal Paginated by Volume
    Hall, Kenneth. "The Role of the Hammond B-3 in the Rhythm and Blues Tradition." *Keyboard Quarterly* 11 (1996): 42–55.

Note: Some journals are paginated continuously throughout an entire year's issues (i.e., by volume)—the first page of the third issue of the year might be numbered 340, for example. In this case, only the volume number and year are required.

Article in a Journal Paginated by Issue
    Ireland, G.W. "The Poet as Scientist in the Work of Paul Valery." *New Criterion* 67.4 (1992): 18–29.

Note: In the case of a journal which numbers each issue separately, include, in addition to the volume number (in this case 67), the issue number (4).

Article in a Monthly Magazine
    Colbert, Zak. "Eating after Midnight: The Best Late Food." *Barbeque Monthly* Sept. 1997: 62–70.

Article in a Weekly Magazine
    Princip, Ruza. "Painting on Silk." *Maclean's* 31 May 2001: 23–26.

Article in a Daily Newspaper
>Kerr, Grant. "Youth Orchestra Soars at Gothic Arches." *The Times-Globe* (Saint John) 21 July 2002: B4+.

Note: If the city's name is not part of the newspaper's title, supply it as above. Specify an edition after the date and before the page reference if the newpaper has more than one. In the example above the "+" after the page number indicates that the article appears on more than one page, but not consecutively.

Book Review
>Sanderson, Heather. "Up to His Old Tricks." Rev. of *Pilgrim*, by Timothy Findley. *Canadian Literature* 34 (1999): 657–660.

Unsigned Article
>"Rebels Retreat into the Hills." *The Economist* 15 Aug. 1988: 34–36.

Note: In the case of an editorial, add the word "Editorial" after the title.

III Sample Electronic Source Entries

Because of both the lack of standards of organization with regard to on-line information and its inherent instability, entries referring to on-line sources need to include kinds of information that those referring to other media do not. The MLA recommends that Works Cited entries for on-line sources contain whichever of the following categories of information are available and relevant (and in this order):

- Name of author, compiler, translator, or editor (last name first)
- Title of a short work within a database, site, or scholarly project (such as the name of an article or a story), in quotation marks, followed by the description "On-line posting."
- Title of a book (underlined or italicized)
- Name of editor, compiler, or translator (if not mentioned earlier)
- Publication information for any print version
- Title of the database, project, periodical, or site (underlined or italicized)
- Name of the editor of the database or project
- Identifying numbers, such as version, volume, issue, or other
- Date of posting or revision
- Name of subscription service; name and location of library
- Name of discussion list or forum
- Numbers of pages, paragraphs, or other sections
- Name of any sponsoring institution
- Date you accessed the site
- Complete URL (in angle brackets); if it has to be divided between two lines, it must be broken at a slash, with no hyphen

Professional Site
> *Douglas Coupland Page.* U of Guelph. 5 Feb. 2001
> <http://www.coupland.uoguelph.ca>.

Article in a Journal
> Friser, Ingram. "The Suicide of Christopher Marlowe." *New Renaissance Studies* 1.2 (1999): 18 pars. 29 Dec. 2001
> <http://newren.quennsu.ca/index.html>.

Personal Site
> Fraser, Iain. Home Page. 28 February 2002 <http://www.inst.regello.it/776>.

Scholarly Project
> *Prison for Women Page* ed. Nancy Helwig. Nov. 1997. McGill U. 22 Aug. 2002
> <http://www.mcgill.ca/P4W/~help/>.

Posting to a Discussion List
> Marquis, Paul. "Tottel's Odd Choices." On-line posting. 31 Jan. 2000 Renaissance Electronic Conference. 1 March 2002
> <http://reneleccon.utoronto.ca/english.htm>.

Article in a Reference Database
> "Jack Bush." *Canadian Encyclopedia Online.* Vers. 99.1.2 April 1999. Canadian Encyclopedia. 16 Sept. 2002
> <http://www.canadiane.com:700>.

Electronic Mail
> Gabriel, Peter. E-mail to the author. 20 June 2002.

Article in an On-Line Periodical
> Baird, David. "The Poetics of Online Travel Information." *Eobserver* 6.2 (1998). 20 May 1998
> <http://www.nyu.edu/english/eobserver/ccd.html>.

Note: Types and formats of on-line information are constantly changing. If you are in doubt about the format of an entry, provide the most specific information you have, following as far as possible the general pattern of MLA entries. Given the instability of on-line information, it is always a good idea to print off any on-line materials you use.

■ Content Notes and Bibliographic Notes

MLA style also accommodates the use of endnotes or footnotes. They may be used to present information that does not fit comfortably into the main text—such as explanatory material, or commentary on sources—or to direct readers to sources. In both cases, insert a superscript numeral at the relevant point in the text, and supply the note either at the foot of the page or after the end of the main text.[1]

Note
1 Additional information on the use of content and bibliographic notes can be found in the *MLA Handbook* 227–229.

Work Cited
Gibaldi, Joseph. *MLA Handbook for Writers of Research Papers*. New York: MLA, 1999.

MLA Essay Format
See the notations on the sample essay (at 9.1) regarding margins, spacing, and placement of elements.

Quotations—Prose
Quotations that run four lines or less (in your paper) are placed in quotation marks and integrated into the text of the essay. Longer quotations are set off from the text; they begin on a new line, and are indented one inch (or 10 spaces) from the left-hand margin. Indented quotations do not require quotation marks. If the quoted material is a single paragraph or part of one, do not indent the first line any more than the standard one inch; if the quoted material includes part or all of a second paragraph, indent the beginning of each paragraph three spaces.

Quotations—Poetry
Verse quotation of three lines or less are placed in quotation marks and integrated into the body of the essay. Designate line endings with a slash (/), leaving a space on either side of it. Longer quotations are set off from the text and indented one inch (or 10 spaces). Indented quotations do not require quotation marks. Reproduce the lines exactly as they appear in the original, duplicating all margins, spacing, etc. If a line of verse will not fit inside the right margin, put the remainder of it on the next line and indent it a further three spaces. If you begin an indented quotation in the middle of a line of verse, position the partial line as it appears in the original, rather than at the left margin, to preserve the appearance of the verse.

Quotations—Drama
Indent dialogue between two or more characters in a play the standard one inch (or 10 spaces). Indented quotations do not require quotation marks. Present the characters' names in all capital letters, followed by a period

(OTHELLO.). Indent subsequent lines by the speaker three additional spaces. For a new speaker, return to the one-inch standard indent.

▌▌▌ Use of the Ellipsis

Minor alterations to the original wording of a quotation are acknowledged through the use of an ellipsis (three spaced periods). In MLA style, an ellipsis inserted by the essay writer is enclosed in brackets to differentiate it from one that appears in the original text:

Original: "Joyce creates a unique connection between the stories in *Dubliners* through his use of progressively older narrators, replicating the course of a human life in the maturation of the perspectives from which the individual stories are told."

Edited version: "Joyce creates a unique connection between the stories in *Dubliners* through [...] the maturation of the perspectives from which individual stories are told."

If one or more periods occur in the omitted material, a fourth period must be added, outside the brackets on the appropriate side:

At the end of a sentence: "and no other evidence was found [...] ."

At the end of a sentence, with parentheses: "was found [...]" (32).

Omitting a sentence: "evidence was found. [...] However, the..."

In the case of verse, if an entire line or more is omitted, insert, in brackets, a line of spaced periods about the length of a typical line of the quoted poem:

> Drive your cart and your plow over the bones of the dead.
>
> The road of excess leads to the palace of wisdom.
>
> [. . . . .]
>
> He who desires but acts not, breeds pestilence.
>
> The cut worm forgives the plow. (2–3, 5–6)

■ 8.2 AMERICAN PSYCHOLOGICAL ASSOCIATION (APA) STYLE

The following information is based on the *Publication Manual of the American Psychological Association*, 5th ed. (Washington, DC: APA, 2001) and on information from the APA Web site (www.apa.org).

Parenthetical References

In APA style, the author–date method is used to cite references. This information is supplied using an introductory signal phrase and/or a parenthetical reference at the end of the quotation, paraphrase, or summary. In the case of a direct quotation, a page reference is also supplied:

> Chapman (1999) noted that "initial research found no correlation between the use of the drug and the appearance of these side effects" (p. 35).

If more than one of these three elements appears in the parentheses, separate them with commas:

> (Chapman, 1999, p. 35)

In the case of a paraphrase or summary, just the author and date of publication are required:

> A recent study found that poverty was becoming increasingly feminized (Sloane, 1997).

> One model, developed by Lee (1989), divided the process into three stages.

Note: You do not need to repeat the year in subsequent references to the source within the same paragraph, as long as this does not create any confusion with other sources.

Two Authors
If the source has two authors, cite both of them every time you refer to the work.

Three, Four, or Five Authors
Cite all of the authors the first time you mention the source. Thereafter, supply only the surname of the first author followed by "et al." ("and others").

Six or More Authors
Cite only the surname of the first author, followed by "et al."

Groups as Authors
If the author is an association, corporation, or other group of some kind, spell out the group's entire name the first time you refer to the source, supplying an abbreviation in brackets. Subsequent references can use the abbreviation:

First reference: (National Association of Orthopedic Technicians [NAOT], 2001)

Subsequent references: (NAOT, 2001)

Works with No Author
If a source has no author, provide the first few words of its reference list entry (usually the title) and the year. Present these identifying words in quotation marks if the source is a short text such as an article or a chapter, and in italics if it is a full-length text such as a book, report, periodical, or brochure:

("Public Policy," 1987)

(*Three Syndromes*, 2000)

Note: If "Anonymous" is supplied as the author, treat it as if it were a name:

(Anonymous, 1992)

Two or More Works within the Same Parentheses
If two or more works are cited at the same time, list the names in the order in which they appear in the reference list, separated by semicolons:

(Hanson, 1997; Latoya, 1999)

Personal Communications
Communications such as e-mail, personal interviews, and discussion group postings are not recoverable sources, so they are not included in the reference list; they are cited only in the text. Provide the communicator's initials and surname and an exact date:

(D.E. Cookman, personal communication, October 1, 2002)

Electronic Sources
If no author is specified, supply a title (as described above in "Works with No Author"). If there is no page number, supply a paragraph number, if available, using either the "¶" symbol or the abbreviation "para." If no paragraph numbers are provided on the site, provide a heading from within the document and the number of the paragraph following it:

(Neurological Disorders, 2000, Conclusion, para. 2)

Reference List
The reference list contains detailed entries for all of the sources you have cited in your essay; these entries provide titles, subtitles, dates of publication, publishers, places of publication, editors, and other relevant information about your sources. Do not include works you may have consulted but have not directly referred to in the essay (a list that includes other sources, and sometimes annotations on the sources, is a bibliography).

Here are some of the essential features of the reference list:

- It appears on its own page (or pages) after the main text of your essay.
- The word "References" appears centred at the top of the page, in the same font and text size as the body of your paper, and in plain text—not underlined or in bold or in quotation marks.
- The first line of each entry begins at the standard left-hand margin, and any subsequent lines are indented. This format, called a "hanging indent," is usually preferred for student papers and published articles; some instructors, however, may prefer the "paragraph indent," in which the first line of the entry is indented and all subsequent lines begin at the left-hand margin—consult your professor to discover which style he or she prefers.

See the References page of the sample essay elements at 9.2.

III Format of Reference List Entries

Order

- The entries are alphabetized by the authors' or editors' last names. If there is no author, alphabetize the entry according to the first significant word of the title.
- Order several works by the same author by year of publication, the earliest first. Supply the author's surname and initials in every entry.

Authors

- Provide surnames and initials for up to six authors; if there are seven or more authors, use "et al." to abbreviate them.
- Use commas between authors' names; with two or more authors, use an ampersand (&) before the final name.
- If you refer to two or more works by the same author published in the same year, arrange them alphabetically by title and add a letter—"a," "b," and so on—immediately following the year in the case of each work: (1999a).
- Spell out the full name of a group author (e.g., an association).

Publication Date

- Give the year of copyright; for magazines and newspapers, add the exact date (month or month and day, as applicable).

Titles

- Capitalize only the first word of the work's title and subtitle, and proper nouns.

- Titles of articles or chapters are presented in standard type, with no quotation marks.
- Titles of nonperiodicals (books, brochures, motion pictures, CDs, computer software, etc.) are presented in italics or underlined.
- Titles of periodicals are presented in full, in uppercase and lowercase letters (i.e., capitalized as they appear in the periodical), and in italics or underlined. Volume numbers are also in italics or underlined.

Publisher

- The publisher's name can be shortened (eliminate articles, abbreviations, and descriptive words like "Publishers," but keep the words "Press" and "Books").
- Give the city; if it is not a major publishing centre, provide also the state, province, or country, as applicable.

Models of Reference List Entries

Book
Author's Last Name, Initials. (Year). *Title of book: Subtitle of book.* Place of Publication: Publisher.

Article
Author's Last Name, Initials., Author's Last Name, Initials., & Author's Last Name, Initials. (Year). Title of article. *Title of Periodical, Volume,* Page Numbers of Article.

On-Line Document
Author's Last Name, Initials. (Year). *Title of Work.* Retrieved month day, year, from URL.

Note: See "Sample Electronic Source Entries" on page 74, which provides more detail concerning the types of information that can appear in a citation for an on-line source.

Sample Book Entries

Book with One Author
Johnson, E.T. (1990). *Psychology and public policy.* New Haven, CT: Fisherbooks.

Book with Two or More Authors
Slater, A.G., Erdminger, E., & Millar, G.L. (1956). *Finding our families.* Oxford, England: McSorley & Son.

Corporate Author
National Association of Orthopedic Technicians. (2001). *A history of orthopedic appliances.* Toronto: Author.

Note: When the author is also the publisher, supply "Author" in place of the publisher's name.

Unknown Author
The basics of encryption. (1998). Wheeling, WV: Datatech.

Editor
Hong, J.L. (Ed.). (2000). *Tell me a story: Oral narratives of the gandydancers.* Vancouver, BC: Tide Song Press.

Encyclopedia or Dictionary
Sadie, S. (1980). *The new Grove dictionary of music and musicians* (6th ed., Vols. 1–20). London: Macmillan.

Entry in an Encyclopedia
Bergmann, P.G. (1993). Relativity. In *Encyclopedia Britannica* (Vol. 26, pp. 501–508). Chicago: Encyclopedia Britannica.

▌▌▌ Sample Article Entries

Article in a Journal Paginated by Volume
Booth, D. (1989). Reading acquisition and family income. *OISE Quarterly, 22,* 88–102.

Article in a Journal Paginated by Issue
Cohen, I., & Lafite, R.C. (1995). Tannin and esters: Some recent research into the chemistry of red wine. *Oenophile, 16*(2), 80–88.

Article in a Newspaper
Burliuk, G. (2002, March 18). You never know what you've got until it's gone. *The Globe and Mail,* p. R1.

Article in a Magazine
Assam, M. (1999, May). Build your own time machine. *Popular Science,* 18-23.

Review
Kelly, M.T. (2001). [Review of the book The new protest movement]. *Geophysical Quarterly,* 20, 280–291.

▌▌▌ Sample Electronic Source Entries

Internet Articles Based on a Print Source
Bowser, J.A., & Wesley, B. (1998). Alternatives to methadone treatment. [Electronic Version]. *Addiction, 33,* 112–120.

Article in an Internet-Only Journal
Davis, P.P. (2000). Patterns in teenage repeat offending. *Psycoloquy, 39.* Retrieved April 20, 2001, from http://uchicago.edu/psycoloquy/00.11.html

Nonperiodical Document Created by an Organization
Hampton County Mental Health Task Force. (n.d.). *Rates of affliction among isolated seniors*. Retrieved December 11, 2002, from http://www.hamptonhealth.org

Note: If no posting or revision date is available, use (n.d.).

Document with No Author or Date
Webtrends 2002. (n.d.). Retrieved September 5, 2001, from http://www.webtrends.org

Message Posted to a Newsgoup
Haffner, G. (2001, December 2). Trends in colour field research [Msg 4]. Message posted to news://sci.psychology.vision

Journal Article Retrieved from a Database
Egoyan, A. (1989). Early studies in cognition. *Journal of Applied Psychology, 56*, 489–496. Retrieved May 15, 2002, from PsychArticles database.

APA Essay Format

See the notations on the sample essay elements (at 9.2) regarding title page format, margins, spacing, and placement of elements.

Quotations
Quotations of 40 words or less are integrated into the text of the essay and are enclosed in quotation marks. Longer quotations are indented one-half inch or five spaces, double-spaced like the main text of the essay, and are not enclosed in quotation marks.

Ellipsis Points
Indicate where you have omitted material from a quotation with ellipses. If the omitted material occurs within a sentence, use three spaced periods (...). If the omission occurs between two sentences, add a fourth period (....).

Page Numbers and Running Heads
Number pages, beginning with "1" on the title page, in the upper right corner of the page one-half inch from the top and one inch from the right-hand edge of the page. Five spaces to the left of the page number, include a running head composed of the first two or three words of your title.

Headings
APA articles use one to five levels of headings. For most essays, three levels should be sufficient:

Centred Uppercase and Lowercase Heading

Flush Left, Italicized, Uppercase and Lowercase Side Heading

Indented, italicized, lowercase paragraph heading ending with a period.

Tables

Begin each table on a separate, numbered page. Type "Table" and its arabic numeral (e.g., 1) flush left at the top of a page. Double space the table.

8.3 OTHER DOCUMENTATION STYLES

Students who use the Chicago and CBE documentation styles can find format information on the Internet at the following sites:

Chicago Style

www.wisc.edu/writetest/Handbook/Documentation.html
mimas.calstatela.edu/library/guides/3chicago.htm
www.library.www.edu/ref/Refhome/chicago.html

Council of Biology Editors (CBE) Style

www.monroecc.edu/depts/librarycbe.htm#single
www.wisc.edu/writetest/Handbook/Documentation.html
www.bedfordstmartins.com/online/citex.html

Chapter 9

Sample Essays

■ 9.1 SAMPLE ESSAY IN MLA STYLE

The short sample essay on the following pages demonstrates both MLA format and some of the organizational and stylistic features described in various sections above. The assigned topic for this paper was "Does Medea satisfy the definition of the tragic hero that Aristotle presents in the *Poetics*?"

Jason C. Cawley

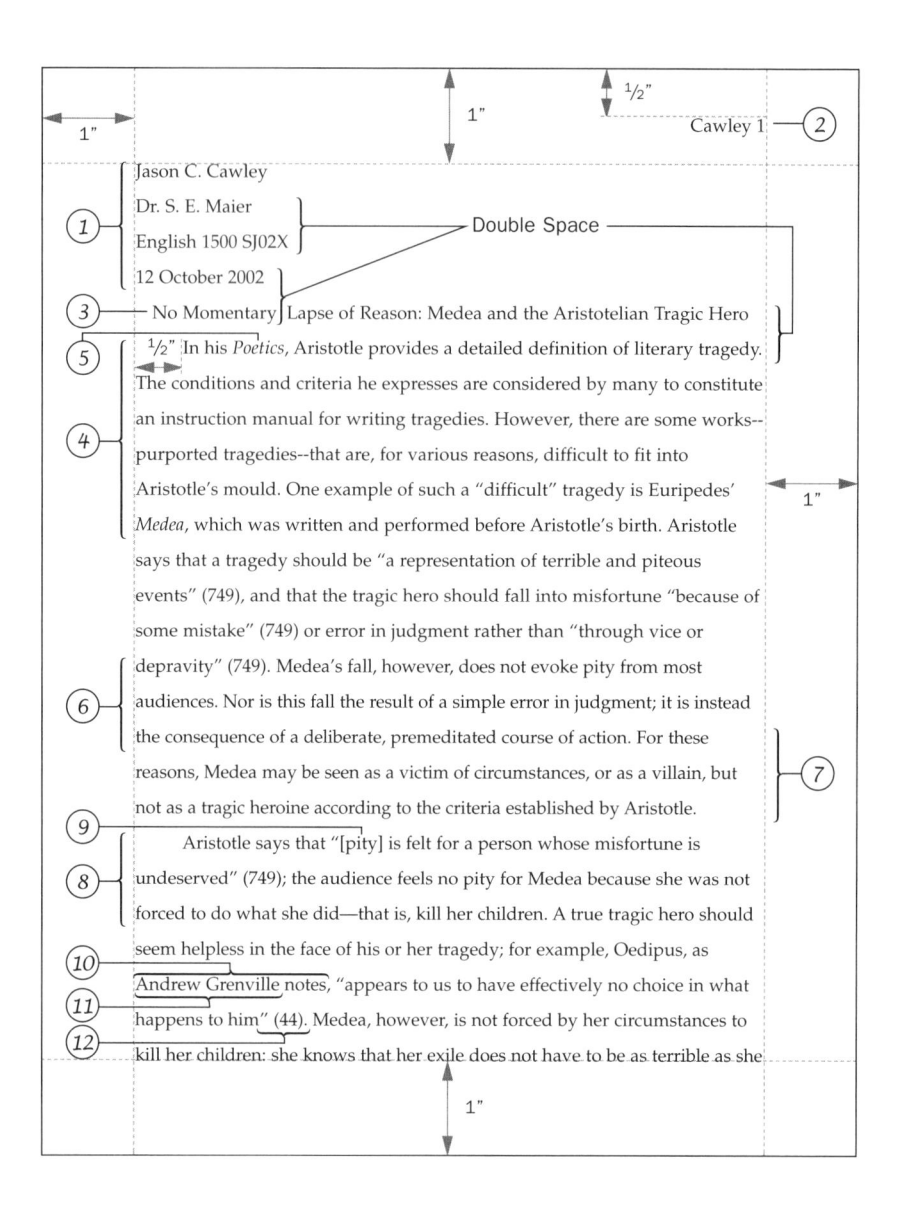

Dr. S. E. Maier

English 1500 SJ02X

12 October 2002

No Momentary Lapse of Reason: Medea and the Aristotelian Tragic Hero

½" In his *Poetics*, Aristotle provides a detailed definition of literary tragedy. The conditions and criteria he expresses are considered by many to constitute an instruction manual for writing tragedies. However, there are some works--purported tragedies--that are, for various reasons, difficult to fit into Aristotle's mould. One example of such a "difficult" tragedy is Euripedes' *Medea*, which was written and performed before Aristotle's birth. Aristotle says that a tragedy should be "a representation of terrible and piteous events" (749), and that the tragic hero should fall into misfortune "because of some mistake" (749) or error in judgment rather than "through vice or depravity" (749). Medea's fall, however, does not evoke pity from most audiences. Nor is this fall the result of a simple error in judgment; it is instead the consequence of a deliberate, premeditated course of action. For these reasons, Medea may be seen as a victim of circumstances, or as a villain, but not as a tragic heroine according to the criteria established by Aristotle.

Aristotle says that "[pity] is felt for a person whose misfortune is undeserved" (749); the audience feels no pity for Medea because she was not forced to do what she did—that is, kill her children. A true tragic hero should seem helpless in the face of his or her tragedy; for example, Oedipus, as Andrew Grenville notes, "appears to us to have effectively no choice in what happens to him" (44). Medea, however, is not forced by her circumstances to kill her children: she knows that her exile does not have to be as terrible as she makes it seem. Knowing that she and the children are to be exiled, Jason comes to Medea, prepared to "make provisions for [her], / So that [she] and the children may not be penniless / Or in need of anything in exile" (449-451). Medea also arranges to have a place to stay while in exile. King Aigeus accedes to the conditions Medea establishes regarding his treatment of her: "That you yourself will never cast me from your land, / Nor, if any of my enemies should demand me, / Will you, in your life, willingly hand me over" (733-735). The children, then, would have been no especial burden to their mother; Medea does not slay her children out of even perceived necessity, but schemes their deaths because "it is the best way to wound [her] husband" (801). After Oedipus' fall and self-blinding, the audience feels sorry for him. After Medea's fall and the murder of her children, she demonstrates an apparent lack of sorrow, saying "my grief is gain when you cannot mock it" (1337) and "The children are dead. I say this to make you suffer" (1345); this arouses in the audience only disgust.

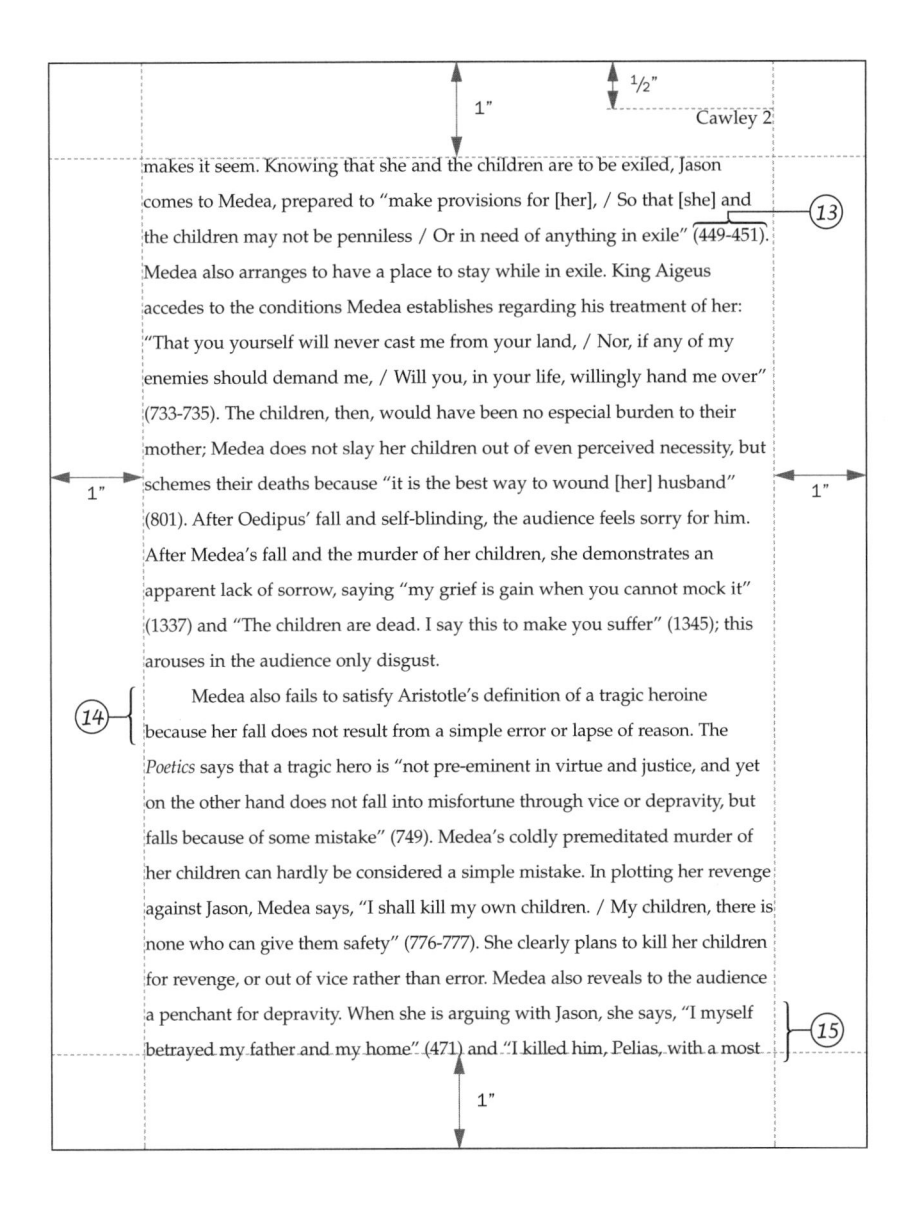

Medea also fails to satisfy Aristotle's definition of a tragic heroine because her fall does not result from a simple error or lapse of reason. The *Poetics* says that a tragic hero is "not pre-eminent in virtue and justice, and yet on the other hand does not fall into misfortune through vice or depravity, but falls because of some mistake" (749). Medea's coldly premeditated murder of her children can hardly be considered a simple mistake. In plotting her revenge against Jason, Medea says, "I shall kill my own children. / My children, there is none who can give them safety" (776-777). She clearly plans to kill her children for revenge, or out of vice rather than error. Medea also reveals to the audience a penchant for depravity. When she is arguing with Jason, she says, "I myself betrayed my father and my home" (471) and "I killed him, Pelias, with a most dreadful death / At his own daughters' hands" (474-475). These actions not only show Medea's untrustworthiness, which is indisputably a moral vice, but they also, as Sara Raftis points out, "indicate an utter disrespect for one of the most highly valued institutions of Greek culture—the family" (23). Kreon, the King of Corinth, says, "I love my country too—next after my children" (326). Medea's disrespect for family—most of all her own—is indicative of moral shortcoming. Her unheroic vice and depravity are revealed not only through the action of the play, but by her history as well.

Because of Medea's perceived moral corruption, she fits more comfortably into Aristotle's description of "an extremely wicked man [...] falling from prosperity into misfortune, [which] might indeed call forth human sympathy, but would not excite pity or fear" (749). The audience can feel no real pity for Medea, who kills her children deliberately and vengefully, rather than seeming to be forced to do so by circumstance. Nor does the audience feel that Medea's suffering is undeserved; indeed, Medea does not even give the audience a sense that she *is* suffering after the deed has been done. Her fall into misfortune is not her exile, because, as the audience sees, she makes provisions for herself in that regard with King Aigeus. Her true fall, which is her murdering of her children, is not brought about because of the "mistake or error of judgment" (749) described in the *Poetics*, but by her own scheming and corrupt nature.

Cawley 4

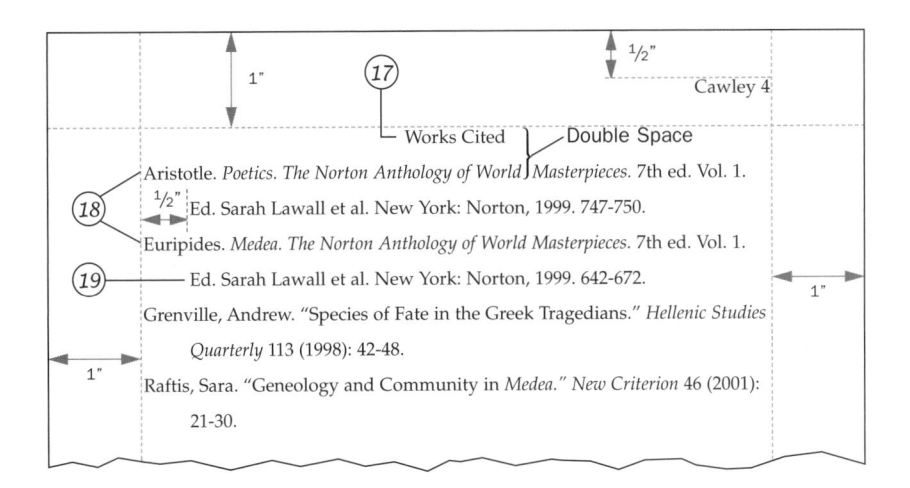

Works Cited

Aristotle. *Poetics. The Norton Anthology of World Masterpieces.* 7th ed. Vol. 1. Ed. Sarah Lawall et al. New York: Norton, 1999. 747-750.

Euripides. *Medea. The Norton Anthology of World Masterpieces.* 7th ed. Vol. 1. Ed. Sarah Lawall et al. New York: Norton, 1999. 642-672.

Grenville, Andrew. "Species of Fate in the Greek Tragedians." *Hellenic Studies Quarterly* 113 (1998): 42-48.

Raftis, Sara. "Geneology and Community in *Medea*." *New Criterion* 46 (2001): 21-30.

■■ Essay Commentary

(1) MLA style does not prescribe a title page. Instead, a block of information is placed in the upper-left quarter of the page preceding the main text of the essay (your professor may prefer a title page).

(2) Use a header in the upper right-hand corner that includes your last name; this guards against confusion if one of your pages becomes separated from the others.

(3) Centre the title, in plain type, immediately above your text.

(4) The writer begins his essay by immediately identifying his subject: Aristotle's ideas on tragedy as they apply to Euripides' *Medea*.

(5) The writer does not need to refer to "the *Poetics*, the famous critical text by the ancient Greek philosopher Aristotle" because he knows that his reader is already familiar with the author and the text in question.

(6) The writer establishes the main subtopics of his argument: Medea's fall does not evoke pity, and it is not the result of an error in judgment. The introduction of the essay's main points can also appear after the thesis statement (see 1.6).

(7) The writer's thesis statement presents a clear, specific response to the question posed in the assignment.

(8) The first sentence of the first body paragraph presents the paragraph's central idea. The writer presents a quotation from one of the texts in question in order to base a specific analytical comment on it.

(9) The writer acknowledges that he has emended the original wording of Aristotle's text through the use of brackets.

(10) The writer introduces a comment from a critic with an introductory phrase that runs grammatically into the quoted material and that establishes the writer's agreement with the quoted commentator ("as Andrew Grenville notes...").

(11) The full name of the quoted author is provided (subsequent references to this critic should include only his surname).

(12) A parenthetical page number is provided following the quotation, outside the quotation marks and inside the period.

(13) Quotations from the play *Medea* are referenced with line numbers rather than page numbers. For a play with several act and scene divisions, such as a Shakespearean text, the parenthetical reference would also include act and scene designations.

(14) The topic sentence of the second body paragraph introduces the second subtopic named in the introduction (Medea's fall does not result from a lapse of reason). It also provides a logical connection to the preceding paragraph ("Medea also fails...").

(15) The writer repeatedly makes specific reference to the original texts in order to support his assertions.

(16) The writer concludes by reviewing the central points explored in the essay, restating his ideas in slightly different terms than he has employed elsewhere in the paper.

(17) The title of the Works Cited list, in plain type, is centred at the top of its own page; the list begins immediately under it (one double space).

(18) The authors' names are alphabetized. If there were an entry beginning with a title instead of an author, it would be alphabetized according to the first word in the title other than *The*, *An*, or *A*.

(19) The second line of the entry is indented (as are any subsequent lines) so that it is easy for the reader to scan the alphabetized first words.

9.2 SAMPLE ESSAY ELEMENTS IN APA STYLE

Title Page

Running head: MENTAL LEXICON: THE EFFECT OF MULTIPLE MEANINGS

Mental Lexicon   1

Mental Lexicon: The Effect of Multiple Meanings
When Searching for Words in the Mental Dictionary
Sheila French
University of New Brunswick

Essay Text

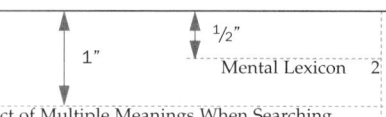

Mental Lexicon 2

Mental Lexicon: The Effect of Multiple Meanings When Searching for Words in the Mental Dictionary

There are two different types of information, *declarative* and *procedural*, contained in long-term memory (Bushnell & Mullin, 1993). Declarative information supplies meaning and facts, such as meanings for words. Procedural information contributes to the carrying out of actions, such as when a person types on a keyboard or drives a car. These two types of information are inseparably linked; however, most research prefers to focus only upon declarative information and how it is encoded, stored, and retrieved (Bushnell & Mullin, 1993).

It makes sense to assume that individual pieces of semantic information are stored in a network (Bushnell & Mullin, 1993). For example, a piece of information like the word "elephant" also encompasses other pieces of information like animal, has a trunk, lives in a zoo, etc. In turn, all of these individual pieces of information can be understood on their own terms and may be linked to other terms. One network model of the way that declarative knowledge is stored and accessed comes from Collins and Quillian (1989). Theirs is a hierarchical model consisting of units, properties contained in each unit, and pointers that link units together.

This model raises many questions. Smith (1990) raised the issue of "how ambiguity affects the organization of semantic information within the mental lexicon" (p. 68). Some, perhaps many, English words have multiple meanings. How are these various meanings represented in the lexicon? It may be that a

Reference List

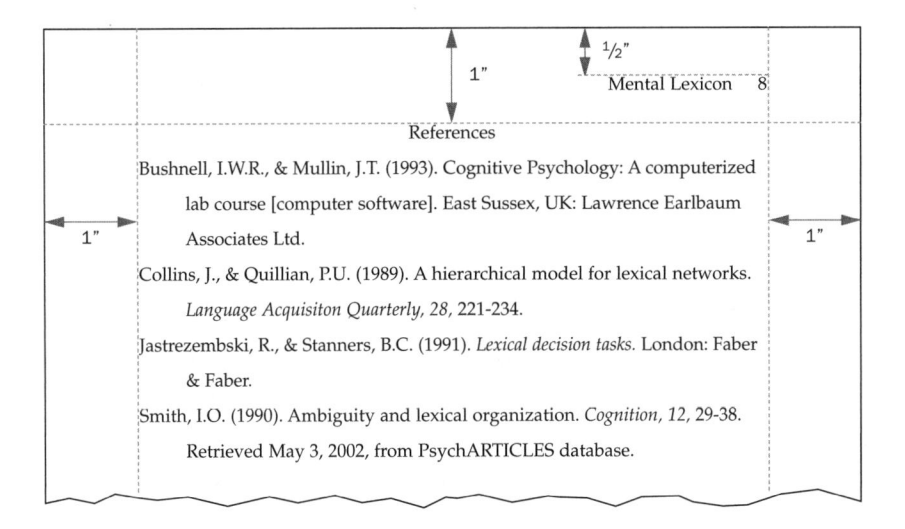

Mental Lexicon 8

References

Bushnell, I.W.R., & Mullin, J.T. (1993). Cognitive Psychology: A computerized lab course [computer software]. East Sussex, UK: Lawrence Earlbaum Associates Ltd.

Collins, J., & Quillian, P.U. (1989). A hierarchical model for lexical networks. *Language Acquisiton Quarterly, 28,* 221-234.

Jastrezembski, R., & Stanners, B.C. (1991). *Lexical decision tasks.* London: Faber & Faber.

Smith, I.O. (1990). Ambiguity and lexical organization. *Cognition, 12,* 29-38. Retrieved May 3, 2002, from PsychARTICLES database.

INDEX

Academic materials, reading of, 12–14
Academic writing. *See* Essays; Writing
Adjectives, demonstrative, 45
Adverbs, conjunctive, 58
Agreement
    between nouns and pronouns, 55–57
    between subject and verb, 54–55
Ambiguous reference, 61
American Psychological Association (APA) style, 77–84
    of verb tenses, 51–52
Antecedents
    agreement with pronouns, 55–57
    compound, 56
    missing, 62
    remote, 62
Anthologies, in citations, 70, 73
Apostrophes, 66–67
Appendices, 12
Appositive phrases, 59
Article entries, cited, 72, 73–74, 75, 81, 82, 83
Audience, 48
Author-date method of citation, 78
Authors
    corporate, 69, 73
    groups as, 78, 80
    in indirect sources, 70
    multiple, 69, 72, 78, 80
    unknown, 69–70, 73, 82
    works with no authors, 79, 83

Bibliographic notes, 75–76
Body, of essay, 39
Book reviews
    cited, 74, 82
    critical, 8–10
Books, cited
    in APA style, 81–82
    in MLA style, 72–73
Business reports, 11–12

Chicago style, 84
Clustering, 19
Collective nouns, 56–57
Colons, 63–64
Commas, 57, 64–66
Comma splices, 57–58
Compound antecedents, 56
Compound nouns, 66–67
Compound subjects, 55
Comprehension, reading, 13
Conclusion, 34, 39–40
Conjunctive adverbs, 58
Context
    of academic writing, 50
    in Introduction, 38
Coordinating conjunctions, 58, 64–65

Council of Biology Editors (CBE) style, 84
Critical/analytical essays, 6–7
Critical book reviews, 8–10

Dangling modifiers, 63
Databases, on-line, 26
Demonstrative adjectives, 45
Dependent clauses, 59
Descriptive essays, 7
Dictionaries, 35, 82
Documentation, 68–84
Drama. *See* Plays

Editors, in Works Cited/References list, 82
Electronic sources
    in APA style, 79, 81, 82–83
    in MLA style, 71, 72, 74–75
Ellipsis points
    in APA format, 83
    in MLA format, 77
Encyclopedias
    as resource materials, 26
    in Works Cited/References list, 82
Endnotes/footnotes, 68, 75–76
Essays
    critical/analytical, 6–7
    descriptive, 7

key terms in assignments, 5–6
planning of, 14–15
purpose of writing, 1–2
rereading the assignment, 32
thinking about, 14–15
types of, 6–12
understanding the question, 32
Executive summary, 11

First draft, 32–33
Format, of essay, 36, 52–53
  APA style, 83–84
  MLA style, 76–77
Freewriting, 19

Gender-neutral language, 52
Grammar, in revision process, 34–35

Headings, styles of, 83–84
Highlighting, 13

Indefinite pronouns, as subjects, 55
Independent clauses, 59
Internet
  directories, 27
  plagiarism and, 24
  for resource materials, 26–29
Introduction, 34, 37–39

Letter of transmittal, 11
Libraries, 25–26
Lists, 60

Main clauses, 59
Mapping techniques, 19
Marked essays, 53

Misplaced modifiers, 62–63
Modern Languages Association (MLA)
  index to resources, 26
  style, 68–77
  verb tenses in style of, 51
Modifiers, 58, 62–63
Multivolume works, in citations, 70

Newsgroups, 83
Newspaper articles, 74, 82
Nondiscriminatory language, 52
Note-taking, 13, 15, 29–31
Noun phrases, 59
Nouns
  agreement with pronouns, 55–57
  compound, 66–67

On-line resource materials, 26. *See also* Internet
Outline
  development of, 18–19, 31
  expansion during research, 31
  first draft and, 32, 33
Oxford English Dictionary (OED), 35

Page numbers, styles of, 83
Paragraphs, 31, 39
  ending, 46–47
  length, 44–45
  in revision process, 34
  structure, 41
  transitions between, 42–44
Parallelism, 45, 60–61

Paraphrases, 22, 25, 30, 35–36, 78
Parenthetical references
  APA style, 78–79
  MLA style, 68–71
Periodicals, indexes to, 26
Periods, 58
Personal communications, 79
Phrases, 59–60
Plagiarism, 24–25, 30
Plays
  citing of, 70
  quotations from, 76–77
Poetry
  citing of, 70
  quotations from, 76
Possessives, faulty, 66–67
Prepositional phrases, 59
Pronoun reference, faulty, 61–62
Pronouns, 45
  agreement with antecedents, 55–57
  agreement with nouns, 55–57
  indefinite, 55, 56
  possessive, 67
Proofreading, 36
Publication dates, 80
Publishers' names, 81
Punctuation, of quoted material, 69

Question, understanding the, 4–5, 32
Quotations, 22, 30, 31, 35–36
  in APA format, 83
  direct, 24, 30–31
  in MLA format, 76–77

Reading
  academic materials, 12–14

comprehension, 13
retention, 13
Reading aloud, 36
Record-keeping, 53
References, 36
Repetition, 34, 46
Reports, 11–12
Research
    establishing needs, 21
    materials, 21
    papers, 10–11
    support material in, 21, 22–24
Resource materials
    assessment, 28–29
    on the Internet, 26–29
    in libraries, 25–26, 28
    locating, 25–28
    note-taking, 29–31
    on-line, 26
    scholarly, 22
Retention of reading, 13
Revision
    checklist, 34–36
    process, 33
Running heads, styles of, 83
Run-on sentences, 57

Scholarship, nature of, 22
Search engines, 26–27
Semicolons, 57, 58, 64
Sentence fragments, 58–60

Sentences
    length and structure, 35
    run-on, 57
    of support, 46
    topic, 41, 46
Skimming, 14
Social sciences reports, 12
Spelling, 35
Squinting modifiers, 63
Style, 49–51
Subjects
    agreement with verbs, 54–55
    compound, 55
    indefinite pronouns as, 55
Subordinate clauses, 58, 59
Subordinate constructions, 58–59
Subtopics, 3–4
Summaries, 8, 22, 25, 35–36, 78
Synonyms, 35

Tables, 84
Thesauruses, 35
Thesis, 31
    common weaknesses in, 17–18
    development of, 14–18
    first draft and, 32
    in the Introduction, 38–39
Title, of essay, 37
Titles, in Works Cited/References list, 80–81
Tone, 48–49
Topic, choice of, 3–4
Topic sentence, 41, 46
Transitional words and phrases, 43–44, 46

URLs, 29

Vague reference, 61
Verbal phrases, 59
Verbs
    agreement with subject, 54–55
    tenses, 51–52
Vocabulary, 50

Web sites, assessment of, 28–29
Word choices, 35
Works Cited/References list, 29, 36
    APA style, 79–83
    MLA style, 71–75
Writer's block, 19–20
Writing, process of, 3, 32–35